Getting Older, Getting Fleeced

Getting Older, Getting Fleeced

*The national shame of
financial elder abuse
and how to avoid it*

by

Pamela Camille

FITHIAN PRESS
SANTA BARBARA, 1996

Published by Fithian Press
A division of Daniel and Daniel, Publishers, Inc.
Post Office Box 1525
Santa Barbara, CA 93102

Book design: Eric Larson

LIBRARY OF CONGRESS CATALOGING-IN-PUBLICATION DATA
Camille, Pamela
    Getting older, getting fleeced : the national shame of financial elder abuse /
    Pamela Camille.
        p. cm.
    ISBN 1-56474-172-9 (ppbk : alk. paper)
    1. Aged—Crimes against—United States—Prevention. 2. Fraud—United States—
    Prevention. 3. Swindlers and swindling—United States—Prevention. I. Title.
    HV6250.4.A34C35   1996
    362.88'084'6—dc20   96-4178
                                                           CIP

for Mom

Contents

Fraud by Friends and Family

Preventing Elder Abuse

Appendix

Acknowledgements

Many people helped me on this project, and most of them helped for no other reason than a deep concern for older Americans. I would like to thank first David Reher, who enthusiastically got the ball rolling. Then there was the tall, handsome detective who must remain anonymous but who gave me my first list of resources (you know who you are; thanks). Thanks also to Susan Aziz and all the FAST people. Thanks to Toshio Tatara and Paul Blunt, and all the APS workers who gave me their time. Thanks to Margaret Stanish, Keith DeVincentis, David Westburg, and Steve Sisolak for their riveting interviews, and thanks to all the people at the banks and stock brokerages who gave me their time. Lastly, I thank Mike and my boys for being so supportive throughout. I love you guys.

Getting Older,
Getting Fleeced

Introduction

The Fastest-Growing Crime in America

WE HAVE TWO OPTIONS: either we die young or we get old. Right now in America the fastest-growing segment of the population is the segment growing older. According to the 1990 census, by the year 2,000—five years away at this writing—there may be 426 million people worldwide over the age of sixty-five. In America today there are 33 million people over the age of sixty-five, and 1990 census projections are that by 2050 over half the U.S. population will be comprised of those forty-three and older.

Baby Boomers' parents are not only aging and dying, but they are being looted. According to 1990's national census figures, 70% of the wealth of our country is owned by those fifty-five and older. That 70% makes a massive money target for all the con artists who would rather steal than work. Some of their scams for plunder take so much energy and creativity that one wonders if they'd be successful working honestly rather than fleecing someone's mother or grandmother. The money they steal, however, is infinitely bigger—and easier—than anything they can do legally. The amounts of money being fleeced, primarily from those over fifty-five, is staggering: $40 billion a year from telemarketing scams alone, according to the FBI's 1994 testimony in the congressional hearings supporting Anti-Telemarketing Fraud Bill (HR 868). Health fraud is costing the elderly about $25 billion a year in phoney health products alone, and insurance and medical service fraud cost consumers another $31 billion in 1994 alone, according to estimates from the National Health Care Anti-Fraud Association.

The purpose of this book is to warn everyone who is getting older: there are legions of criminals out there who want to steal the money you have worked hard to earn and save. I will tell you who to be prepared for, what kinds of scams are being run, and how to avoid them. You are not being protected by law enforcement, although law enforcement has begun a massive campaign against those who plunder the elderly. Law enforcement's awareness of the problem is in the early stages, and the problem is too vast for them to really have it under control at this point. At the moment, for example, a con artist can take you for $1 million, and since he or she won't use a gun to do it, the most time they'll ever do behind bars is eighteen months, according to federal sentencing guidelines. At least nine times out of ten, once a con artist gets your money, no matter how hard the FBI and your state's Attorney General fight to return it to you, you will never see that money again.

Although there are dedicated warriors battling to change things, white-collar crime against the elderly pays in America, and it pays big. I will tell you about the network of con artists across the country who share "suckers lists," so that if you are fleeced once by one variety of con artist, your name is passed to other con artists. This network of con artists is so monied and extensive that the con artists own some of the most sophisticated computer and communications systems in the world. They are also brilliant psychologists, according to David Westburg, a U.S. Postal Inspection Service supervisor who's been cracking interstate con-artist rings for seventeen years. "They are the smartest, most successful psychologists in the country." In his opinion, your only weapon against them is knowledge.

Sadly, the above information only protects you against 70% of the fleecers. According to Toshio Tatara's issue paper "Elder Abuse in the United States" for the National Aging Resource Center on Elder Abuse, 30% of those who abuse the elderly—and this includes all forms of abuse, not just financial—are the sons and daughters of those victims. Everyone over forty should have a completed, detailed living trust in a safe place that will prevent this tragedy. I will also give you the many other reasons you should have a living trust. I will give you resources and resource centers to help you obtain this vital document. I will also tell the loyal, honest sons and daughters how to discover whether your parents have already been hit by con artists—and what to do if they have. The warning signals are definite and clear, as the con artists' modes of operation all share the same patterns.

With knowledge, we can all be empowered enough to stop the many varieties of con artists—from the gypsies who marry then poison the elderly to get their money, to the telemarketers, the health-care con artists, and the home equity con artists. In order to research this book, I spoke to detectives, attorneys general, and criminal investigative accountants in every corner of America, and all of them agree: financial exploitation of the elderly is the fastest-growing crime in America.

Con artists read the obituary columns, so they know when bereaved spouses are at the most vulnerable point in their lives. They also read every document coming from the probate courts, so they not only know what you're worth, and whether or not the courts consider you competent, they know a plethora of intimate things about your dead spouse. And they use that knowledge, ruthlessly, to get to you. Widowers are hit almost exactly as often as widows, and with the same tragic results. It is only because there are more widows that the widow figures are slightly higher than the widower figures. The most recent studies by the National Aging Resource Center on Elder Abuse prove conclusively that men are every bit as vulnerable as women to these con artists.

The day you turn fifty-five or lose your spouse, you should be prepared for the inevitable barrage of con artists who want your money. Prepare a thorough defense that covers every potentially vulnerable aspect of your life—from building a rich social network to combat your loneliness, to organizing your own safe, financial investment system. Get ready, then, to build your fortress against the bad guys!

The Landscape of Exploitation in America

Exactly how fast is the crime of financial exploitation growing? As an example, in Nevada alone the number of reports of financial exploitation of the elderly for 1994 was up 250% over the 1993 figures as reported by the Nevada Division for Aging Services. In Florida, the state holding the largest percentage of those over sixty-five in the country—18%—the number of reports for 1993 soared after the establishment of an 800 number, Central Abuse Hotline. Anonymous reports can be made in Florida whenever any citizen suspects elderly abuse, and reports are then given to the districts in which the abuse allegedly occurred. Adult Protective Services then investigates.

According to Margaret Dixon, APS Medical Health Care Program Specialist in Florida, for 1993 the number of reported financial exploitation cases in her state were as follows: improper management of finances, 2,448 cases; coerced transfer of assets, 2,443 cases; resources depleted through treachery and deceit, 726 cases. The total comes to 5,617 unsubstantiated reports, which is a rather high number when compared with the California totals for the same period—1,383 cases, as cited by the California Health and Welfare agency. It is interesting to note that California does not have the same anonymous, toll-free hotline as Florida. A study done by the National Aging Resource Center on Elder Abuse (NARCEA) confirms that states that have a mandatory reporting law have twice as many elder-abuse reports as states that don't have such a law, and I'm sure that when studies are completed, equally astonishing contrasts will be made between states that have central hotlines and states that don't. In a preliminary report by NARCEA, reports on elderly abuse nationwide are up about 20% on average.

These figures certainly reflect increased awareness. Seniors are beginning to shed their shame and stand up for themselves. More elders report these days, although still not enough. When I spoke on the phone with Lea Pearson, the assistant manager of the Criminal Justice Department at the AARP in Washington, D.C., she warned me, "Don't depend too much on figures. I don't believe them, because the elderly are too ashamed to report. When it's their own kids who beat them or take their money, the parents think it's their own fault for being bad parents. They somehow think they deserve this treatment. Or they feel ashamed because they were stupid to get taken in by a con artist. They're embarrassed. They don't report." Unfortunately, figures from the Senate Subcommittee on Health and Long-Term Care, Select Committee on Aging's report, "Elder Abuse: A Decade of Shame and Inaction" (1990) substantiate Lea's claim. "The subcommittee noted that elder abuse is far less likely to be reported than child abuse and estimated that only one out of every eight cases of elder abuse is reported." A problem that goes hand in hand with the lack of victims' reports is the victims' unwillingness to press charges against a family member or trusted friend—those who most often exploit them. Another problem is the difficulty in reclaiming stolen goods or assets.

Nevertheless, impassioned Adult Protective Services workers and other social workers are reporting for them. States with mandatory reporting laws for bankers, and even states with voluntary reporting laws for bankers—all with legal protection against libel suits for those making their reports "in good faith"—are experiencing more reports to Adult Protective Services from banks suspecting fiduciary abuse of elders. The same is occurring in stock brokerages across the nation. We will see even more changes in that direction as banks and brokerages are held culpable in some exploitation cases. As law enforcement and the financial and legal communities band together with Adult Protective Services, exploitation cases are being handled more efficiently. Civil suits are recovering money and assets, thanks to new laws enacted in many states.

Growing media attention is also building awareness on all sides. As victims are identified as intelligent, fully capable victims of highly professional con artists, the stigma of stupidity is lifted from other victims, and they are coming forth. As we are made more aware of the intricacy and brilliance of some of these con artists in action, the rest of us have stopped saying, "Oh, I would never fall for that!" We would, because the con artists are that good. With or without statistics, one thing is certain: as the elderly population expands, so does the abuse against them.

Because the number of elderly is greatest in certain regions, this book will concentrate on those areas. According to the 1990 U.S. census, California has the largest number of citizens over sixty-five, more than three million. Florida has the largest percentage of its population—over 18%—over sixty-five. Nevada is the third hotbed of financial exploitation of the elderly in the United States. According to the 1994 National Real Estate Association figures, Nevada is the fastest-growing state in the United States, and many of the newcomers are retirees. Nevada also has Las Vegas, the telemarketing fraud "boiler room" capital of America, which loots primarily the elderly. Why Las Vegas? FBI case studies have shown that even when the actual base of a telemarketing scam business is in Massachusetts or upstate New York—as two FBI-targeted operations were—they still use a Las Vegas post office box and bank account. Apparently, says Margaret Stanish, Deputy Attorney General of Nevada, telemarketing con artists are

more successful when using the "lure of Las Vegas." Las Vegas—the
original gambling mecca of the United States—is an almost mythical
place where you can get rich quick. In Las Vegas, the myth goes, you
can become a millionaire overnight. Say "Las Vegas" to many seniors,
and they envision dancing girls, glamorous celebrities, and instant
riches. Con artists use it because it works.

Although these three states are the largest targets for con artists,
there is no state untouched, and some other states do get specialized
treatment from con artists. Arizona, for example, was the primary target for a massive health fraud scam. Each state deals with exploitation
crimes differently, and I will highlight those differences. Each state is
plagued with financial exploitation, and many of the smaller states' innovative measures can be used as learning tools for the other states.
When I attended a national conference of Adult Protective Services
workers I heard horror stories from representatives of each state.
Where there is money, there are rip-offs, and many poorer districts'
representatives told me, "In my district, the main reports we get are of
the offspring stealing their parents' Social Security checks to buy
drugs or booze." Sadly, you don't have to be rich to be vulnerable.

The elderly have always been treated badly, but in earlier centu-
ries people usually died before they got too old; they didn't have to
endure abuse for long. America, from the beginning, hasn't really
known what to do with older people. A New Jersey law written in 1772
required a search of entering ships for old people, "lest they come
ashore and become a burden to the community." Not that things were
too much better in Europe, from which many of our founding fathers
hailed. Poor widows were driven out of communities and forced to
move around from town to town, the objects of fear and derision. In
England, according to Guy Ragland Phillips in *Brigantia*, "when an old
woman begins to dote and becomes chargeable to a parish, she is generally turned into a witch." Witches, of course, were burned, and
many of the "witches" were nothing but poor old women.

Indeed, as is pointed out by Reginald Scot in *Discoverie of Witchcraft*, rich witches were made saints by the Pope, while poor witches
were burned. In history, then, to be old and poor was a death sentence; to be old and rich could at least get you canonized—and here,
I assume, it helped if you bribed your local bishop.

Whether you are poor or rich, if you are over fifty-five years of age, there is someone sniffing around, trying to steal whatever you have. The maximum figures gathered from the National Aging Resource Center on Elder Abuse indicate totals of all forms of elderly abuse—physical, sexual, neglect, abandonment, mental suffering, and financial—affect 10% of the population over sixty—or roughly four million Americans a year. Financial abuse comprises 25% of that figure, or one million Americans a year, according to S.K. Steinmetz's article "Elder Abuse" in the January–February 1981 issue of *Aging*. Paul Blunt, an Arizona attorney specializing in elderly exploitation cases for the last five years, disputes that 25% figure, citing a much higher percentage of financial abuse emerging from a recent study in Canada. He feels that once seniors come out and really report, financial abuse figures will soar.

"We're at the tip of the iceberg," says Mr. Blunt. "In Canada's most recent study, financial abuse has been shown to be the fastest-growing form of elder abuse, and I think the same is happening here. My guess is that it will become clearly the largest form of elder abuse."

Partly because I agree with Paul Blunt, I have put together a list of as many resources as I could unearth. The good news is the huge number of resources and the passion of the people who are working to stop abuse of our parents and grandparents. For those of you who are "officially poor," there is a large pool of free legal aid service resources in your area. For those of you who are on fixed incomes, collecting social security—in other words, too rich for the free services, but too poor for private attorneys—through the National Academy of Elder Law attorneys you can avail yourselves of *pro bono* or reduced fee services through local bar organizations. You need organization names, and local services to contact. You need preparation and education now, before your money is craftily stolen.

Interview with Toshio Tatara, Ph.D., National Center on Elder Abuse

I met Toshio Tatara in San Antonio at the Adult Protective Services conference, which he is responsible for organizing each year. He introduced me to everyone he could think of who might help me in my research on financial exploitation of the elderly. Among the countless

APS workers I spoke with, everyone's eyes brightened when his name was mentioned. Tatara is a well-liked man, and he returns the affection.

"I am an ordinary man," he said when I told him I admired all the work he's done in the fight against elder abuse. "They [the APS workers] are the real heroes. They are the ones on the front lines every day." He told me to call him "any time, if there is anything I can do. This is so important. I guess I could go back to Japan and be a wealthy businessman; but this work for the elderly is much more important. Call me any time. I'm old, so I don't need to sleep."

Taking him up on his offer, I interviewed him by telephone at 11:15 p.m., his time, from the West Coast. I began the interview by asking him about the National Center on Elder Abuse and its history, as well as its function.

"Can you tell me about your position as Director of the National Center on Elder Abuse and what you do?"

"The purpose of the National Center on Elder Abuse is to develop and disseminate elderly abuse information to the public."

"What do you do?"

"We do different organizational assignments, quarterly newsletters. We do literary research on elderly abuse, and we do training on aging matters for Adult Protective Services. We provide technical assistance on aging. We compile best-practice models and distribute them to APS and other organizations. We do a lot of data collection, collecting data from different state Agencies on Aging and from the University of Delaware, where they have a huge research center on aging. We also conduct activities for the National Association of State Units on Aging. I am also the Director of Research for the American Public Workers Association. We're not a law-enforcement agency, but we work with the law enforcement agencies from time to time."

"You're very busy."

"Yes."

"How long have you been in the elderly-abuse field?"

"Since 1984. I come from the child-welfare field. I am still involved in foster care and adoption for them. I've been involved with the American Public Workers Association since 1976. Before that I taught social welfare."

"How did the National Center on Elder Abuse begin, and why?"

"The Administration of Aging in 1988 used their money—$1 million over three years—as dictated by Title IV of the Older Americans Act, which mandated national resource centers on aging, so it was created by legislation."

"Have you seen positive changes in the area of financial exploitation of the elderly?"

"Positive changes are occurring, but as technology progresses, new crimes come along. Telemarketing is an example. But more states are aware of the problem, and they have become prepared. There is more legislation. By adding financial exploitation to legislation clauses, more criminals can be apprehended. APS and law enforcement agencies are becoming more sophisticated in apprehending criminals, but criminals are always one step ahead of law enforcement, it seems.

"The best defense is prevention: elders must become educated consumers. Everyone around the elders must also become more educated."

"Do you think there is more financial exploitation now than before, or is there more awareness?"

"It's hard to say. I think exploitation has always existed, but when life was simpler, crime was simpler. We are catching more criminals. Elders are becoming better educated and more aware. They are more ready to report now. Even today, though, the fear of reporting is great. Elders are very defensive. Frail elders are very afraid they'll be put in nursing homes."

"Do you have a vision about this country's future with regard to financial exploitation of the elderly?"

"For the first time in this country's history, in 2020 older people will make up the majority of the population. Right now, there are forty-two million elderly, and sixty-seven million people under the age of eighteen. In 2020, the child population will decline, but there will be thirty million more elderly than now—seventy-two million. Legislation will change. It will have to! Public transportation will have to change, and better financing of Medicare, Medicaid, and Social Security, along with other programs. The elderly will be using more resources, but there will be fewer workers to finance them.

"Most of the wealth—70%—will be in the hands of the elderly, as it is now, so con games can only increase! The most vulnerable people will have all the money. The elderly will be the targets of all kinds of crimes. How to prevent it? Education! The elderly must have the courage to report when victimized. There is no shame. It is the only way."

Two Heartbreaking Stories

> Your eyes are widely open flowers.
> Only their centers are darkly clenched
> To conceal Mysteries
> That lure me to a keener blooming
> Than I know
> And promise a secret
> I must have.
>   —ALICE WALKER
>   *In Search of Our Mothers' Gardens*

Alice Walker wrote this beautiful poem in honor of "...the old people—male and female—who persist in their beauty in spite of everything." Her grandfather, who was eighty-five years old, "...looks at me with the glad eyes of a three-year-old. The pressures on his life have been unspeakable. How can he look at me in this way?"

A startled, elegant woman enters the Nevada courtroom where she has been asked to testify. She is sworn in, and tries to keep her eyes on the lawyer who is questioning her, but she wants to see the defendant, so her eyes find him. Her eyes are sad when she looks at him. Although her life's savings are gone, she is not angry. She cares for him. Her testimony about the con artist who fleeced her out of her life's savings—about $250,000—is very painful to hear. She is a nice woman who loved her late husband. About the swindler sitting in the defendant's seat, she says, "I thought he and I had so much in common. I told him my late husband was a Presbyterian minister, and he told me he had also been a Presbyterian minister. I told him my husband always wanted to take care of me, and he said that's what he wanted, too, to take care of me. I still can't believe he ever meant to harm anyone."

The defendant was quite a charmer, and she'd been his eighteenth victim. Unfortunately, in this case the money is gone. The lovely widow whose husband left her "comfortable" financially will have to depend on federal and state aid programs for as much as the next thirty years. (She is sixty-eight, and, although weary emotionally, she is in perfect health.) The man who took her money, along with millions of dollars belonging to another seventeen elderly victims, was sentenced to a mere three years in a Nevada state prison and was out on parole in just one year. Conning and fleecing is the only way he has ever supported himself, and it is doubtful he will develop new job skills. In fact, it was while he was out on bail for fleecing another group of victims that he moved to a new city and fleeced these latest eighteen elderly victims.

The state of Oregon recently battled successfully for Amelia deGremli, a brilliant writer-scholar who had directed a theater group in Nevada. When she suffered a serious stroke and could no longer speak or move much, Charles and Carole Dutton, the son and wife of her close friend, legally obtained power of attorney and took all her money. They sold her house in Nevada and bought a new one in Oregon, without telling her friends where they were taking her. They moved Amelia into an Oregon nursing home and paid its $825.00 monthly fee out of Amelia's $1,000 Social Security check. They never spent a dime so Amelia could have toiletries, clothing, or field trips from the nursing home.

With considerable effort, Amelia managed to scribble the word "HELP" on a postcard and mailed it to a good friend in Nevada. Authorities in Oregon were notified, and an investigation began. The Duttons, now living in the house purchased with proceeds from the sale of Amelia's Nevada home, spent Amelia's considerable savings on cars and furniture. They wore Amelia's jewelry, and escaped without consequence. As was the case in much of the country until recently, Oregon's laws made it impossible to get criminal convictions on elderly financial abuse cases. They were deemed "family matters," and the power of attorney, though grossly abused, had been obtained legally by the Duttons. (This may bring to mind previous attitudes toward domestic violence, also deemed "a family matter" until public outcry demanded laws be changed.)

Fortunately for Amelia, her court-appointed conservator filed a civil suit, and the Duttons were ordered by an outraged judge to repay all of the $46,644.03 they'd diverted from her savings account, as well as all the money from the sale of her Nevada home. He slapped an extra $50,000 fine on the Duttons for the suffering they caused Amelia.

The laws and attitudes toward financial exploitation of the elderly are changing. Finally, heroes are emerging to recover assets stolen from the vulnerable elderly by ruthless criminals. Most often, these criminals are people their victims knew and trusted implicitly.

All over America, in cities and towns, awareness of financial exploitation of the elderly is blooming after years of shameful silence. Jeanine McCullough, an ombudsman for the Area Agency on Aging in southern Oklahoma, described what moved her to fight for the rights of the elderly. When she was ten years old, in 1969, a horrific crime was committed in her area, and, as she said, "I learned that you could beat up an old person, set their house on fire, take all their money, and never go to jail, because 'it's a family problem.' I decided I had to do something about that." She and her dedicated co-workers have organized southern Oklahoma into an active elderly abuse awareness center. Law enforcement in southern Oklahoma doesn't dare react to an elderly abuse report as "a family matter" these days!

America is a country growing older, and the over fifty-five group is being fleeced faster than any other group. Many con artists specialize in robbing the elderly because they have studied their weaknesses. It's simple: people over fifty-five have the money or the home equity, and they're vulnerable. Their physical handicaps or at-home retired lifestyles have left them isolated, and con artists know exactly what these people long for at this stage in their lives. The con artists deliver—the trustworthy lines, the kindly friendship, and removal of all worries—magnificently. Through telemarketing scams, real estate and stock scams, through becoming the victims' "sweet young befriender" or "new best friend," con artists are looting the elderly of this country. Some of the fleecers, of course—29%, according to the National Aging Resource Center on Elder Abuse—are the victims' own sons and daughters.

The criminals fleecing the elderly are sophisticated, and use sophisticated tools. One con artist, for example, had a computer print-out of all recent widows in Illinois. When he approached them, each had been a widow for exactly three years. After tirelessly collecting data, he'd discovered that three-year-widows were the most susceptible to his telemarketing scheme. He fleeced several widows before being apprehended.

I have met hundreds of crusaders from all over the country who are fighting this mushrooming crime. The victims' stories are heart-breaking, but the victories these crusaders have won is inspiring. Hoping to share the knowledge I gained through working on this project, I started a lively discussion group in my home. Several ripped-off seniors have come to my home to share their experiences, losses, and victories. They are beautiful, funny, smart, dignified people who have worked hard for decades. Financial success and self-reliance are all they've ever known, and they now suffer deep shame at their victim status. However, they are me a few years from now, and they have absolutely nothing to be ashamed of. The criminals are very good at what they do, and we are all vulnerable.

My hope in writing this book is to alert and empower readers before the same crimes happen to others. I hope to reach the middle-aged who are still in the workforce, as well as the vigorous newly retired seniors. By acting now, you can secure your financial future. By organizing your finances, your futures, as well as your hearts, souls, and friendships, you can become less vulnerable. Your home will remain your haven, and the money you earned in your youth will belong only to you.

I learned first hand that financial exploitation of the elderly is life-threatening—and does kill—when I was nine years old. My best friend's grandma had a huge mansion in Bel Air, where movie stars and basketball players live. My brother and I would run through the mansion, gleefully enjoying the endless rooms. No one ever found anyone when we played hide and seek in that house! We were enthralled by the house's elevator that soared upward three stories. There was an intimate dining room on the third floor, and the elevator was in the kitchen; the butler could get food from the kitchen to the intimate party without the food getting cold. For this nine-year-old and her seven-year-old brother, "Grandma Jane" (not her real name) and her estate were better than any fairytale queen and her castle. She loved us, and invited us to come any time we liked. The seven-mile bike ride on our stingray bicycles was well worth the treat, and we visited her often that summer. The year was 1962.

Grandma Jane invited my little brother and me to a grand wedding she was hosting on her estate, and we could not believe our good fortune. Our mother was also very excited—she, as our "driver," was allowed to attend the affair, Jane's butler had informed her on the phone. She dressed us in what my brother referred to as "foo-foo garbage sissy clothes" and drove us through the huge iron gates to the valet who would hide our car behind all the Rolls Royces. Mom was agog at the sight of the mansion. "You kids didn't exaggerate, for once," she muttered, and Mike and I giggled at each other.

The grounds were like a dream: there were yellow-and-white striped umbrellas, lavish flowers, and gorgeous people everywhere. My brother and I were quickly lost in the jungle garden trying to chase a deer. We'd discovered yet another fantastical part of the estate.

When we suddenly escaped the dense jungle of ferns and exotic flowers, we found Jane presiding over the wedding reception. She was delighted to see us, even though we were terribly muddy. (My mom was with her and was not so pleased with our scruffy condition.)

"There you are!" Jane shouted, opening her arms expansively and bidding us come and be hugged by her. It didn't matter a bit that we were covered with mud and grass stains. She was the most beautiful woman I'd ever seen, with lush brown hair and crisp blue eyes. She stared at me a few minutes and said, "Pam, you're going to be a beautiful woman someday."

No one had ever said anything like that to me before; in fact, my older siblings often worried aloud about my hopelessly gawky appearance. What a magical experience for me to hear a magnificent queen bestowing the promise of loveliness on me! I blushed and hugged Jane hard. "Thank you so much!" At that instant I silently swore to myself that I would never forget her, although there was no real reason at the time to make such a vow.

Only two months after the wedding, however, my best friend (Jane's granddaughter) told me tearfully that her parents were in court, trying to save Jane's home for her. I went to my friend's mom and demanded some answers. I was shaking with rage, and she spoke to me as an adult.

Jane's daughter, a beautiful woman in her twenties, sighed and said, "Yes, Pam, we are fighting my brother in court. He says my mom—Grandma Jane—has become senile, and he's trying to take away her home and all her money."

"What!" I shrieked. "How can anyone say that? Grandma Jane is perfect! Why doesn't she just go to the judge and talk to him? He'd see in one minute her mind is perfect!"

Jane's daughter smiled at me and ran her hand through my hair. "My mom really loves you and your little brother, you know. I'll tell her you're ready to do battle for her." She sighed again. "My brother told the judge about the wedding. The wedding cost one hundred thousand dollars, and it was for her gardener. My brother says only a senile woman spends a hundred thousand dollars on her gardener's wedding, and I'm afraid the judge agrees with him."

A hundred thousand dollars in 1962 may have been more than the gross product of a lot of municipalities, but "so what!" I shouted. "Her gardener is like a son to her! It's her money! God, her place is like a national park, it's so big, and he's worked for her for like fifteen years. Who cares? Why can't she do what she wants with her own money?"

"Because my brother is greedy. He wants the money for himself. Oh, Pam, Jane's going to really need us, now. My father built that house for her, and that's all she has left of him. If she loses it, she'll just want to die."

That is exactly what happened. Within a few months, the grand estate and everything in it was sold. The servants who had been considered part of Jane's family were dismissed, and Jane was placed in a tiny expensive-but-sterile apartment without so much as a potted plant on the veranda.

I kept my silent vow to Jane, and my brother and I stopped in to see her every single day on our way home from school. (Her apartment was right on the way home.) When I first saw her, it was a terrible shock. It had only been a few months since the wedding, yet her lovely brown hair was now snowy white. Her crisp, clear eyes were glazed and foggy, and vibrantly alive Jane was now a woman who needed twenty minutes of coaching to recognize us.

After we'd been visiting Jane every day for one month, she, who had once chased us all over her many-acred estate, was bedridden. I'll never forget the day "Jim" (the gardener—not his real name) came to see her. He was leaving when Mike and I arrived, and he was sobbing into Jane's lap. Jane was sitting in a wheelchair, and she stared blankly at us while Jim cried on her lap. She did not know who he was.

In another month we were told Jane had died in her sleep. I was heartsick, but glad it was over for her. I made my mom take us to Jane's funeral just so I could glare at Jane's son through the whole service. He was a murderer, as surely as if he'd put a gun to her head—which would have been kinder. He now had all the money, and looked it. Ten years later I heard from my neighborhood friend that most of it was gone.

Had Jane and her late husband set up a living trust, they could have declared exactly who they wanted to be their guardian, should they ever be declared incompetent. Jane was not incompetent, but if a probate court decides you're incompetent, it behooves you to have someone you can trust to manage your affairs. Had a living trust been set up, Jane could have named her daughter or an impartial bank president to manage the estate. The estate would have been managed according to the couple's pre-specified wishes, and Jane would have lived her life the way she and her husband intended.

Home Equity Fraud

Home Equity Fraud Defined

HOME EQUITY FRAUD is a frequent, common crime committed against mostly poor, older people of color. It is especially horrific because con artists are unscrupulous enough to take the homes of people who have little else. It has been happening in Boston, Atlanta, and Los Angeles for three decades, but the media and dedicated lawyers have waged an all-out war against this crime. Knowledge is still our main weapon, and it is urgent that citizens realize how easy it is for con artists to steal their homes.

Many older people bought their homes decades ago for a fraction of what they are now worth. If the homes are not entirely paid off, as many of them are, there is very little money still owed on homes that the owners have been paying on for, say, thirty years.

Here is a simple example of home equity and its appeal for those who steal. Fred and Jill, an imaginary couple, bought a house in southern California in 1946—when so many people did—for $16,000. By 1986, after a careful, simple life, they've been able to pay off their home. They own it free and clear. Their improved, well-tended, $16,000 house is now valued at about $240,000, so the house's equity would be $240,000. Because of its 1990's value, if they went to a bank and asked for a loan based on this equity in their home, it would probably be no problem to borrow almost $200,000. The bank knows it could get $40,000 more than that if it were to sell the house after Fred and Jill reneged on payments. To the fleecers, then, Fred and Jill are sitting on $200,000 cash—and they want it. Professional home-equity fleecers engage crooked loan companies—they are abundant—who help them take the equity from older couples—indeed, even

31

force them from their homes.

Both Fred and Jill are retired and live at home. Their health is not quite what it once was. Fred, who once took pride in being able to make all home improvements and repairs himself, can no longer get up and down ladders. For the first time in their lives, they'll have to hire outside help to get a new roof and have the house exterior painted.

Enter the home equity fleecer, who poses as a godsend: the ultimate handyman. Surprisingly to me, he doesn't offer a very good price—in fact, in the cases I've researched, his prices were outrageously high—but he charms Fred and Jill. He puts them at ease. He tells them he'll throw in extra services at no extra cost to them, just because they are special and he likes them. They remind him of his own grandparents. He knows how much they must hate shoddy work, because he can see by the beautiful care they've taken of their home what perfectionists they are. He spends three hours chatting with Fred and Jill, during a time in their lives when no one spends three hours at a time with them. Their grown kids are too busy, the doctor's office is jammed, but this very nice handyman gives them his entire afternoon. When it comes time for the couple to sign the papers, they don't read carefully enough to realize they are signing a grant deed to their own home. With one signature, they stand to lose their home.

I spoke with three attorneys who specialize in rescuing victims of home equity fraud. They love their jobs, because they save people's homes—and lives. It was both inspiring and invigorating listening to such fired-up, committed saviors, and I found their insights on prevention and elimination of financial abuse of the elderly to be invaluable.

A Woman Who Wins Against Home Equity Con Artists: Joy Simmons, Legal Aid Foundation of Los Angeles

The first attorney I interviewed was Joy Simmons, who is the senior attorney with the Legal Aid Foundation of Los Angeles. For nine years she ran the Homeowners Outreach Unit, which dealt solely with home equity fraud/theft. She knows home equity fraud; she fights it, and she's been winning battles against it for a decade. A vibrant, beautifully elegant woman, she welcomed me into her office. I asked her what she would like to stress as we began the interview.

"Hmm," she began, and the wheels started whirring in her head. "The ease with which the perpetrators function, and what an absolute plague the crime of home equity fraud is in our community. One of my cases involved a woman in her eighties who owned her home free and clear. Its value was $175,000. One day she received in the mail a property tax bill with someone else's name on it as the owner. She called and went to the tax collector's office, where she was told, 'You don't own this property any longer.' She came to me at the Legal Aid Foundation, and I did a title report on the property. Six or eight months prior to all of this, someone had forged a grant deed on the woman's property. They'd gone to the stationery store, filled out a transfer, and forged it. The crook—we'll call her Jane Doe—then went to the bank and got a loan on the property, maybe $60,000. Jane Doe had made some payments on this loan, so I was able to easily open up an investigation. Jane Doe got nervous and transferred title back to my client. I was able to contact the title insurance company and get the $60,000 loan taken off. It was easy because we caught Jane Doe so early, and she had made some payments on the loan.

"The title company paid the bank, and all seemed well until we realized that, because property had changed hands, taxes on the property had been reassessed. My client could in no way afford the new taxes on her property after the fraudulent transfer, so I had to get the tax assessor to accept the old amount of taxes—$300—rather than the new amount, which was $1,500. It took eight months of wrangling with them, and even then it was not over. Four years later, my client got a notice in the mail from the tax assessor's office saying, 'Your taxes are delinquent. Pay up or lose the property.' It took almost a year to straighten that mess out. And my client was not the only victim. It seemed Jane Doe went to church with my client and some other elderly women whom she'd eventually robbed in the same way. So I was really pleased to end it and win free titles back for my clients."

"What, in your opinion, makes the elderly especially vulnerable—besides, of course, the equity they've built up over the many years they've owned their homes?"

"I think their lack of finances or someone reliable to counsel them. The clients who come to the Legal Aid Foundation often live near the poverty level. Their financial problems have already forced them to take out loans on their property, so they can't afford legal help. And then sometimes 'befrienders' gain the trust of senior citizens just so they can rob them."

"With so many cases, how do you determine where to put time first?" I asked.

"I put in the extra hours for my most stressed clients. Please remember that stress of this kind can and does kill the elderly, so I fight hard and fast. In many of my cases, the liability and fraud are so clear that I can easily get them resolved without a lawsuit. So many things can go wrong while you're waiting for a lawsuit that I do everything I can to restore title without a lawsuit."

I asked, "If home equity fraud and exploitation of the elderly has been going on so long in South-Central L.A., why is it just starting to get national attention? After all, the Homeowners Outreach Center began operating in the late 1970's because of all the home equity fraud complaints. That's almost thirty years."

Simmons grew angry. "Many people in South-Central L.A. are poor, faceless, and minorities. Nobody cared much about this crime until it started happening on the affluent side of town." I shuddered, hoping Simmons was wrong, but I knew she was right. In the late sixties the people getting fleeced in South-Central L.A. were all black, poor, and not well educated. Nobody cared.

"Are you able to get some of the repeat offenders locked up who have exploited so many of the South-Central elderly?"

"Absolutely not. Law enforcement is not getting them off the streets. Everyone knows who the con artists are, but they never get locked up. I sent many cases to the City Attorney because the D.A. wasn't doing anything. Well, the City Attorney talked to the D.A., there's a certain protocol and nothing gets done. One scammer was brokering loans, just taking the money the bank was supposedly lending to someone else. One year later, after everyone had been saying, 'Let's get this creep in jail,' I found out that the real estate board was about to give this guy a real estate license. I had *everyone*—even a reporter who had done a story on this guy—call and write letters to the real estate board to stop him from getting a license. In that case, the right hand didn't know what the left hand was doing." (The "left hand" of the California real estate board Simmons referred to had just finished disciplining this particular con artist for charging illegally high interest rates and excessive loan fees.)

What Simmons said reminded me about Kevin Merritt, because I'd read the shocking article about him in the July 1989 issue of the *L.A. Weekly*. Kevin Merritt owns several real estate-related companies and has ruthlessly fleeced hundreds of people out of their homes. Charles Walker, a former employee of Merritt's, even testified against his former boss, saying, "It was standard procedure to lure financially troubled homeowners into transferring title to their homes by means of misrepresentation and deceit."

"I can't believe this. Tell me more."

"I can tell you about the fads that sweep through the area, threatening people's homes. There was the water-purification fad, where many people were conned into getting purification systems they couldn't afford. Missing one payment nearly lost them their homes."

"Yes, I read about the water purification scam in the 'City Times' Sunday magazine of the *L.A. Times* article in March 1993." That scam had targeted immigrants from countries where the tap water is especially bad, so these people were used to needing water filters. Unfortunately, the immigrants didn't understand enough English to know they were signing away their homes for these outrageously expensive filters.

"Then there was the satellite-dish scam. As an example, there was an older woman who owned a home with a rental unit in the back. Her tenant wanted a satellite dish, since she didn't get cable in her area, so the satellite dish company got the old woman to sign the agreement for her tenant's dish. Her signature automatically placed a lien on her property. When her tenant moved, the tenant naturally stopped making payments on the dish, and the satellite company began foreclosure on the woman's home. I got to them fast and hard with the facts about the tenant's rights, and they took the dish down."

I looked at Simmons and smiled. "You really enjoy winning, I can tell."

She smiled a very beautiful smile. "I love my job! I save people's homes, and I save lives!"

"What can you say about ending this crime? Any visions for the future?"

"First of all, banks and lending institutions need to *be there* for their community. They need to make small loans at reasonable prices. Many banks make no long-term loans to old people, because old people die. The elderly have to go to terribly usurious lending institutions—God, I've seen rates as high as 63% annually! And 35% is not uncommon. Some banks have no qualms about buying these loans from the unscrupulous hard-money lenders. The banks call them 'dream loans.' It's wrong."

"It's hideous. Do you have some other remedies?"

"Yes. I'd like to see law enforcement take a more effective, active role. We've been trying to educate the community, and it helps, but then they go to the police and say, 'Someone else's name is on my property.' The police say, 'It's a civil matter, not a criminal matter,' so these crimes don't get prosecuted. Threats of civil lawsuits do not deter these criminals. They're so rich that their attorneys get them off. Jail *is* a deterrent. I'd also like to see the Department of Real Estate become more of a consumer-protection agency. Heated-up publicity is good, because when home equity fraud happens to sophisticated people who know how to make a fuss and won't let it go, then we get somewhere.

"Until there is a bigger, more cohesive pattern of addressing the problem," Simmons continued, "the problem can't be solved. I've saved a lot of homes and lives, and I love every minute of my job. Absolutely every minute, because there's such a clear delineation between the good guys and the bad guys. I represent the good guys."

Home Equity Fraud Across the Nation

Throughout the country, the media have been very successful recently in addressing the problem of financial exploitation of the elderly. Partly due to all the recent publicity of home equity fraud—"Prime Time Live" had just aired a segment on home equity fraud in South-Central Los Angeles entitled "Stealing Home"—the Los Angeles District Attorney recently announced to the press that he was increasing his staff to include home equity fraud specialists, and that he expected many more criminal prosecutions as a result.

For the majority of elderly people, the home is all they have; it's their only major asset. Any of us who have made mortgage payments and begun to collect memories in our family home can imagine how devastating it would be to lose that home.

"More than a few elderly couples have committed suicide over losing their homes this way," says Robert Youngdahl, Deputy District Attorney for the City of Los Angeles. "Not only will they never be homeowners again, but they'll probably be priced out of the rental market."("Home A-Loan." *Insight,* July 1991.)

The problem has mushroomed all across America. In Massachusetts, the state legislature placed a four-month moratorium on foreclosure on the homes of people who claim to be victims of an equity scam. Five thousand cases were affected. In Atlanta, a private attorney won a large civil suit under the Racketeer Influenced and Corrupt Organizations Act against a family of real estate shysters. The bank that funded this family's crimes is also being sued.

Perpetrators of equity fraud often fleece many victims before local authorities nab them. In Charlotte, North Carolina, legal aid authorities received seventy-five complaints against one home equity loan dealer in one year—a local record.

As Joy Simmons pointed out in the previous section, discrimination is part of the problem. In 1989, a Federal Reserve Bank of Boston report confirmed that the city of Boston's banking policies often excluded residents of Boston's black neighborhoods; there were, in fact, *no* financial services available to these people of color.

It is the elderly who have catastrophic, expensive hospital bills or ancient roofs that must be fixed. These sudden expenses eat up their mortgage payments, and their small retirement or social security checks are not enough. They need loans. Many of these people are not aware of federal truth-in-lending laws, which state that no one may be discriminated against, so when a bank turns them down, they go to a hard-money lender. If the lender is unscrupulous—and many are—he will write up a loan specifically designed so that it can never be paid off. Then the lender will get a home with lots of equity for very little money. These lenders happily rip off the only thing those residents in hard times have: their homes.

I spoke on the telephone with Norma Nordstrom, who is the Deputy Regional Services Administrator for the Department of Public Social Services in Los Angeles. She works closely with law enforcement on cases of financial abuse of the elderly and is a key member of the award-winning multi-disciplinary team FAST (Fiduciary Abuse Specialist Team). She urgently stressed the importance of holding mortgage companies, banks, and lending institutions accountable for the inexcusable loans they are granting and selling.

This is beginning to happen, and will probably happen more. Attorneys are suing banks in Atlanta, Boston, and Santa Monica for not looking deeply enough into loan legitimacy before either lending or buying loans. In Chicago, two banks were forced to settle with 6,750 homeowners who claimed to have been scammed by home improvement companies funded by the banks. Still, the incentive is certainly there for banks to buy outrageous loans. The Virginia-based Consumer Bankers Association says 12% of national banks buy second mortgages from small lenders. After all, a 14% or higher interest rate is very good incentive!

Banks and lending institutions, then, will be held more accountable in the future, and more criminal prosecution will deter some scammers. The brunt of the responsibility, however, will remain with you, the homeowner. In the following chapter I've collected many suggestions from the experts on how to avoid home equity scams. Familiarize yourself with them, and don't let this unspeakable crime happen to you.

Justice for Victims
Bill Flanagan, Bet Tzedek Legal Services

Bill Flanagan is the Director of Litigation for Bet Tzedek Legal Services in Los Angeles, and has been for seven years. The words "Bet Tzedek" are Hebrew, and mean "House of Justice." Flanagan's office floor is lined knee-deep with file folders stuffed with data on each of his many cases. Most of these are home equity rip-off cases, and the ones he showed me all involved elderly victims, cases he won or feels he will win.

Flanagan is wonderful to talk to, partly because he's very intelligent, but also because he speaks with poetic passion about the elderly of this country getting fleeced. And he's funny; when I asked him how he wanted me to introduce him in this book, he waved his hands expressively and murmured theatrically, "He was tall and Redfordesque in his appearance."

I asked him exactly what Bet Tzedek is, and he said, "It's a legal aid office representing poor people in civil cases. It was founded originally by Jewish lawyers to serve poor Jewish people in this very ethnic part of L.A. Now the funding comes from federal, state, and local sources, so we represent everyone." He smiled. "The name was beneficial in one case. We were dealing with a group of Israelis who were scamming the elderly in a bunch of home equity rip-offs, and when they saw that our clients were represented by Bet Tzedek they got pretty nervous."

One of Flanagan's successful cases against a group of home equity rip-off artists was publicized on the television show "Prime Time Live," and I asked him to talk about it. He did so in a way that really brought home to me how vulnerable we all are.

"Here's a woman in her late eighties, almost blind, with hearing problems. She's an African American woman who received her master's degree in Education from USC in 1946. Do you know how tough that makes her? Think of it. I look at you," he said, gesturing toward me, "and I see a strong, independent, intelligent woman. That," he said fiercely, "is what could make you vulnerable when you're older. It's what could make us all vulnerable. What makes us vulnerable is our desire to be independent. Old people want control over their lives. Who doesn't? This woman was determined to live alone despite her handicaps. That isolated her. Think how driven she must have been to earn that degree back in '46. She had her color and her gender going against her, but she was driven.

"Now," he continued, "this crook, who happened to be an Israeli, spent three hours with her. Three hours! No one had spent three hours with this woman, not in years. Do you know what effect that must have had on her, that someone was willing to spend three hours with her? After those three hours, he was in, and this is common. Serial home improvement scammers often become befrienders." (I asked, and, no, this woman had no children or husband.) "This guy got her to agree to a bunch of home improvement loans with his crooked finance company. A legitimate loan company would never finance these loans. There's no way she could ever hope to repay them! No, these finance companies want the house. The typical scenario goes like this: home improvement scammers get the victims to sign over the deed to the house. Then they take out loans on the house."

"What about the finance companies in these cases? They sound so culpable."

"Yes. They must all face consequences if there's going to be any change. I'm suing the mortgage broker and the realtor in another couple cases." He pointed around the room at all the stuffed file folders. "Look at all these home equity fraud cases! We have three lawyers just at Bet Tzedek doing nothing but home equity fraud cases. And why not? Why would anybody go to these poor areas to steal TVs, when they can get $170,000 out of someone's house?"

I mentioned Joy Simmons' comment about racism being a factor in the lack of prosecution. His admiration of Joy was obvious as he agreed with her. "Of course. The guys ripping off poor blacks don't dare go to Beverly Hills to try it, because they know they won't get away with it up there. No, they go where they know they can get away with it.

"But that's changing. There *must* be consequences if this thing is ever going to end. These guys come in the dark of the night to rob these people, and as I was walking down the hallway of the courthouse for this one home equity trial, I looked at all the jurors and thought to myself, 'Finally, in the light of day, in the light of the courtroom, they will face consequences.'"

Bill Flanagan has been so effective in cracking one ring of home equity robbers that when the bad guys hear that Flanagan is after them, they back down and restore title to the owner immediately. This happened recently in a typical home improvement scam: an elderly man needed a new roof, and the same Israeli group Flanagan had battled before got the man to sign over his home to them. The bad guys then borrowed $100,000 against the house, but backed down immediately upon hearing that Flanagan was involved.

How to Protect Your Home: Attorney Kurt Eggert Goes Over the Basics

Down the hall from Bill Flanagan is Kurt Eggert's office. Eggert is a staff attorney at Bet Tzedek and has won some well-publicized cases.

He feels very strongly for his clients—many of them incapacitated or elderly adults—who are grossly exploited financially.

"People see the elderly or incapacitated person and figure, 'They're gonna die soon anyway.' The victim in his nineties is treated much worse than someone in his seventies. There's the 'lying in wait' deed, where a home improvement con artist gets an owner to sign a grant deed and figures, 'When they die, I get the house.' This happens a lot."

"What would you say is your most important piece of advice for people who need to make repairs on their homes and don't want to get into this kind of trouble?"

"Make sure that if you sue the contractors, you can collect money from them. Make sure the contractors you hire are licensed, bonded, and insured. Make sure they're bonded for the specific job you want them to do. If you want your roof fixed, make sure they're bonded for roof repair. If you need a loan, make sure the lenders have assets, so you can sue them if anything goes wrong. If you hire an attorney, make sure that attorney has malpractice insurance. Protect yourself."

"I've heard that you've been in the struggle to make lenders act more responsibly in this. Is that true?"

"We've been fighting to get a law passed saying that lenders *have* to determine that borrowers have the ability to repay a loan. If one of these elderly clients who can't possibly pay gets a loan, the bank or lender should be held accountable. We'd also like to see real estate laws change, but California was paid for with real estate, so changes in real estate laws are hard to make here. Con artists use real estate licenses, because in California if you want to lend money at more than 10% interest, you can do so with a real estate license. I'd like to see that situation get tightened up."

"Any other ideas on problems and solutions?"

"Homeowners need to keep current with their property tax bills. If you don't receive a tax bill at the appropriate time, look into it immediately because something is wrong. The sooner you get to the problem, the easier it will be to fix.

"I think you can relate a lot of this to what's happened to the family in America. Old people don't have relatives looking after them. In other countries, grandparents live with younger generations. They take care of each other. The other thing is the emphasis by law enforcement on violent crimes and drugs. Someone who robs a liquor store of forty-five dollars will go to jail long before some con artist who steals an old person's home. And it takes money to prosecute property fraud cases, which sometimes get complicated. L.A. County's District Attorney got some cash from title companies, who get killed by forged deeds, and other money from County Recorder filing fees. More money, more prosecutors. Some good should come of that. Lenders should be helping out, but too often they just don't care. They have title insurance, so they're protected, and why worry about the poor homeowner?"

I left Eggert's office with a stack of shocking reports on financial abuse of the elderly, but also with some good ideas on avoiding it.

Home Repair and Improvement Without Rip-Offs

Before you begin to look for workers to improve or repair your home, you should be aware that there are groups of home repair con artists as big as one hundred strong who prey on older people. The largest of these groups is referred to as "the travelers" by law enforcement. They are all related to each other, and they move across the United States—moving to warmer climates, for example, when home repair is not sought in the east and north. While one of them is on your roof doing shoddy work, another will be inside your home robbing you. At best, you'll get a miserably poor repair job. At worst, you'll lose your valuables or even your home. Therefore, as much as it sounds horribly complicated to get safe, reasonable, quality repair on your home, please take some extra steps to protect yourself.

The goal of most home equity improvement criminals is to get your home or, at the very least, to use the equity in your home to secure large loans for themselves. Home improvement con artists' most common method is to talk a homeowner into signing a trust deed or grant deed to secure the work they're supposed to do. It is very important to know the difference. A trust deed reflects a loan for a product or service that is secured by the value of the home. A grant deed to a home is just like the pink slip to your car: once it is signed, the holder can take possession. Usually, the con artist does not allow the homeowner to read these documents. Nor does the homeowner get a copy. It seems incredible that anyone could be so ruthless as to slip a grant deed to an elderly person to sign away his or her home, but con artists are, and they do.

The first rule, then, is do not sign anything. Have an attorney read a document first, or two or three people who are good with documents. And, just so you know, any document with the words "trust deed" on it will say that if you can't make the payments on your new roof, carpet, or water filter, you could lose your home. Pretty expensive carpet. Never, ever sign a grant deed unless your attorney is present. You are giving away your home when you sign it.

Avoid using your home as collateral to service repairs. (See the following chapter on other ways you may be able to finance repairs.) It's better to have a leaky roof than no roof at all! Remember also that it is the law that if you buy something for more than twenty-five dollars, you have three days after signing in which to change your mind. Never forget that, and never allow yourself to be pressured.

After using the following guidelines to find a licensed, bonded contractor, get three estimates. Estimates are free, and you'll be amazed at how much estimates can vary in price. To find the contractors:

To begin your search for a contractor figure out exactly what kind of work needs to be done. You will need a contractor who is bonded specifically for that job. There are roofing licenses, chimney licenses, tile licenses, and you must be sure that the person you hire is bonded for exactly the job he is contracted to do. If the work you need requires plumbing, electrical, painting, carpet, and tile, then you need a licensed general building contractor.

Get recommendations from friends and relatives who have recently had the same kind of work done. In my neighborhood, all the homes are about the same age, and we're all on friendly terms. We automatically saunter by and ask a neighbor getting a roof who he hired, how much he is paying, and all sorts of other nosy questions no one seems to mind answering. A happy customer is generally pleased to show off the good deal they got on good work. If that doesn't pan out, try the yellow pages. Any contractor listed in the yellow pages must have a valid contractor's license number included in his ad. The ad will describe all the types of work the contractor is licensed to do.

After arranging for your free estimate, ask the contractor for addresses of houses he or she has worked on. These references are essential; you can see how good the contractor's work is. Good contractors are proud of their work, so if they hesitate to give you names and addresses of other clients, don't use them.

The most important thing to remember about contractors is that good ones never have to solicit business. Never use anyone who comes to your home soliciting business! Some con artists have used the line, "I was driving by and noticed your property doesn't comply with building codes. I can fix it for you." Wrong! Others have dropped in, saying, "I finished a job around the corner, and I have some leftover materials. I can give you a real deal." It sounds great, but a good contractor always has leftover materials and so many other jobs to hurry to that he or she doesn't have to hustle to get rid of them!

Once you have found a contractor for your job, contact your state's licensing board and ask the following questions about your contractor: What kind of work is he or she licensed to do, and how long has he or she held that license? Is the contractor in good standing, or have there been complaints filed or disciplinary action taken against him? What is the name and bond number of the company that insures the contractor's work? Just one phone call containing these questions will give you lots of free information and will make you feel safer.

After that phone call, it's always a good idea to call the Better Business Bureau. Ask them if there have ever been complaints of any kind made against this contractor. Ask what the complaints were, and take notes. That's what the Better Business Bureau is there for, to protect you against unscrupulous businesses. Use it.

Now that you have all this information about your contractor, ask him exactly how long it will take to finish your job, and what kind of warranties he has for his product and his work. Never take his word for it; a warranty must be in writing.

Another vitally important reminder: it is not a good idea to let a contractor offer you financing of any kind. Tell the contractor politely that you will take care of your own financing. A contractor's financing may be on the up-and-up—and may not—but it will be much more costly than the financing you'd get at a bank or from one of the sources I've recommended in the next chapter.

After you've found some qualified contractors, get three estimates on your job. You'll be surprised how much they can vary. The estimates should have everything clearly spelled out, on paper, in easy to understand language. Both labor and materials should be included. Beware of any bid that is substantially lower than the others.

Unlicensed contractors are often cheaper, but it is not wise to hire them. A licensed contractor knows state laws, requirements, and local building codes. He or she can get building permits with greater ease. If you deal with a licensed contractor, you can trace his or her history and work through the licensing board. He or she is insured for injuries on the job. And, if everything goes awry, as Kurt Eggert said, they have the resources to make things right. In other words, you can sue them.

When it comes time to sign a contract, raise your antennae! Never sign until you feel certain you understand every word. If there is fine print, get a magnifying glass. Don't fake it. Also, don't be afraid to cross out parts of the contract you don't agree to. Ask the contractor to initial your changes. It's a good idea to call your local senior center, if you have no one else, and ask when free legal advice is being given. Take the contract to the senior center and ask the volunteer to go over it.

A home improvement contract should include the following: your property's correct address, as well as the contractor's correct address; the address of the state contractor's license board; and a complete description of every single bit of work you wish to have done, and the exact price for each. If specific materials are to be used, they should be listed. If subcontractors will be used, they should be listed. The date work is to begin and the date work should be completed should both be specified. The method and schedule of payments, showing the amount of each payment, should be given. Progress payments are good for you, because you only pay for work that has actually been completed. If a down payment has been agreed upon, that should be spelled out clearly. Money paid to a contractor should not exceed 10% of the value of the work performed on the project at any time. Retention money refers to the money you retain until the job is complete; its purpose is to give the contractor extra incentive to complete the job. The contract should state that the contractor will secure all necessary permits and inspections. There should also be a statement that the completed work will meet all building codes, and that you'll be supplied with all completed inspection reports and permits from local building inspectors when the work is completed. There should be a statement that the contractor and all subcontractors will be covered by workers' compensation insurance. There should also be a statement that no extra work or changes in the contract will be permitted unless authorized by you in writing. Make sure it's in the contract that "cleanup" is to be thoroughly completed by the contractor, and specify the date everything must be cleaned.

Licensed contractors are also required to give you a notice stating that under the Mechanic's Lien Law, they have the right to enforce a claim against your property if you don't pay them.

Remember to get a copy of the contract, and remember also that you have three business days in which to cancel the agreement.

Financing Home Repairs Without Endangering Your Home

In most cities across the country, there are "city improvement programs" designed to improve the appearance of the area. If your home and your financial situation qualifies, you can become part of this city improvement program. The financial terms are unbeatable, but there are many different kinds of arrangements, so you have to go over them carefully. The first thing to do is call your city planner and ask if and when your area will be eligible for a "revitalization project" or "re-development," or whatever they might call it. Cities use various names for these projects, but your city planner should get the basic idea that you're asking whether there is any kind of revitalization project being funded for your area, now or in the future. You then want the planner's office to take you through each step necessary to discover all the types of giveaways and loans available, and what you must do to qualify for them. (Believe me, you will earn every penny of whatever financial break you're given to improve your home.)

As an example of how good such programs can be, my girlfriend was newly divorced, with four school-age children. She was attending college for her post-graduate degrees so that she could become more employable, and had no income except alimony and child support from her former husband. Her house was in the least developed part of the county, and her house was easily the scruffiest in the area. It took a great deal of paperwork for my friend to sort everything out, but the county eventually paid for the entire renovation of her dilapidated home. If you discover that your home is just outside the boundaries for current renovation projects, ask whether the city agency involved could make a waiver of requirements for someone living outside the currently designated area.

Again, in every city of every state in America, there are different programs, requirements, and funding available, but I'll try to give you a general idea of them to get you started. Various types of loans will be offered by your city, but they should fall somewhere in the following categories.

Deferred Loans In most cities there is financing available that requires only that you repay the loan for the home improvement upon the sale of your home. This type of loan is available only to those in lower income groups, but it may be a way for you to stay in your home. This type of loan will put a lien on your home, to be paid upon the sale of your home, so your home's sale price will have to reflect this extra amount. You do not have to make monthly payments under a deferred loan program.

No-Interest Loans In this type of loan you will only repay the principal sum you borrowed. There will be no interest added. You will have to make monthly payments, but they'll be based on the face value of the loan. For example, if you borrow $10,000 and you have 120 months to repay the loan, your monthly payments are calculated by dividing the $10,000 total loan by 120 months, requiring monthly payments of approximately $84.00. This is another kind of loan that is also intended for low-income applicants.

Low-Interest Loans Many cities across the nation—especially in older, more tired areas in the east, north, and south—offer funding for renovations to low-income families for as little as 4% interest. Check with your local city planner's office to see what the maximum household income allowable for this type of loan is. In some cities in the west, for example, where property values are high, a family of four earning $30,000 might qualify. But each city is different, so do your research carefully. It is also important to remember that if you own a piece of rental property and you rent primarily to low-income families, you may be eligible for some of these city improvement programs.

The last thing I'll say about city sponsored programs is that many cities across the nation provide free services to low- and moderate-income families. These may include termite inspection, an architect's assistance in designing major improvements to your home, property inspections to determine damage and the needs of your home, and a list of licensed contractors of good standing in the community. The city may also provide you with free financial counseling to help you choose the best method of paying for home repairs, as well as help in obtaining contractors' bids and on-the-job inspections of contractors. This can be invaluable to people who are not physically able to climb onto their rooftops to see if a job's been done properly. In my own case, I wouldn't know a good roofing job from a bad one, anyway, so, let the city come out, at no cost to you, to make certain your job is being done in a professional manner.

In many cities across the country, if you qualify, your city's housing program will even come and paint the outside of your home. If you have already contracted with someone to do the job but you don't feel secure about the contract's fine print, ask your city planning office or housing authority if someone could come out and read the document before you sign it. You will be amazed by the number of people happy to help you, so if you run into one or two useless, crabby souls, move on until you find good people who want to help you. They do exist.

There are also special city improvement programs available to you if you are handicapped, so look into those. If you are poor enough, the city will provide you with free handiworker service—up to $500 worth of free labor, in many cases! Get to work, then, discovering what is available to you, and act upon that discovery.

If you are not poor enough to qualify for city programs, you may still be eligible for other discounted loans. If you're a member of the AARP, it is always good to give them a call, as they try to help seniors get discounts in every conceivable area of life. They'll also tell you where to start researching.

Whatever kind of loan you get, however, please try to avoid contracts with balloon payments. A balloon payment means that the entire balance of the contract is due in full on a certain date. This balance is huge and, for many people, impossible to pay. Don't agree to it.

Other kinds of loans available are:

Personal Loans A personal loan is a small amount obtained from a bank, credit union, or finance company that is unsecured. This is good, as it places no lien on your property, but the rates for unsecured loans are high. Many life insurance companies will also lend you the equity in your policy at a very low interest rate, but remember that the face value of your policy is reduced by the amount of the loan which is outstanding. Bank credit cards and stock brokerage accounts have a cash amount you can borrow without prior approval. Stock brokerage loans tend to charge lower interest than bank credit cards for these loans, but they are both easily obtained. With the credit card loan, your credit card will be charged each month, and with the brokerage account loan, your monthly statement will reflect the interest charges each month.

FHA Title I Improvement Loans The Federal Housing Administration (FHA) of the U.S. Department of Housing and Urban Development (HUD) backs certain home improvement loans. FHA insures the loan obtained from a private lender for 90% of the total loan amount. FHA requires no trust deed for loans under $7,500, and there is no prepayment penalty. You can't use an FHA loan to put in a swimming pool, but loans can be made for remodeling, room additions, plumbing, electrical work, and roof repair and replacement.

V.A. Loans If you are a veteran who has served in any of the U.S. armed forces, contact your state's Veterans Administration to see what kinds of loans they offer to qualified borrowers. V.A. loans always carry substantially lower interest than other loans, and the terms are excellent.

Financing Through a Contract I cannot urge enough caution on this one, but some wonderful contractors have arrangements with lending institutions that enable them to offer financing for home improvements. The contractor brings you the application and credit contract to complete. The contractor then sells the contract to a third party. This is usually a lien sales contract, which means a deed of trust will be placed on your house to secure payment of the loan. Please exhaust all other means of financing before taking this option! If you feel okay with it, get an attorney volunteering time at your local senior center—or some other legally knowledgeable person—to go over the contract with you before you sign it. The same goes for an equity loan. Avoid it; it is backed by a second trust deed.

Refinancing In refinancing all previous mortgages are paid off in full and one single mortgage is written at current interest rates. You must pay the cost of the new loan and possible prepayment fees on the previous mortgage. If you refinance, you should be prepared for a substantial increase in the amount of your monthly payments.

The Community Reinvestment Act is a federal law that requires the Federal Home Loan Bank Board to review the performance of lending institutions in meeting the credit needs of low- and moderate-income neighborhoods. The Board has established the Office of Community Investment to administer a large fund of money available at low interest to financial institutions as an incentive for lending in low- and moderate-income areas. You can find out about this program in your area by contacting either your local Federal Home Loan Bank Board office, or by calling your local savings and loan association office.

Before You Go to a Lender: Interview with a Lender

Bob Blaney helps run B & C Mortgage, Inc., a small mortgage company in Lake Tahoe that services both California and Nevada. He says that when seniors come to him in the midst of a hardship, he advises them to consider selling their homes. He reminds them if they would buy condominiums, there would be less maintenance, and the proceeds from the sales of their homes would give them cash, so they wouldn't be in debt.

"For some of them, this is emotionally not an option, but I advise people in this situation to look realistically at all of the possibilities. Because, frankly, private equity loans are quick and dirty. Most private equity lenders don't care. They want to know one thing—what is the equity backing the loan? If it's high, they'll make the loan, and they'll slap high interest rates and fees on it. The whole basis of reverse mortgages and home equity loans is profit for the lenders," he reminded me.

I asked Blaney for his advice to seniors regarding things to watch for when going to a lender. He laughed. "If a person wants to believe in you, he'll believe in you. It's that simple. Sometimes, if these private equity lenders don't ask the questions of 'how are you going to pay for this loan?,' it's a done deal. When the seniors don't pay off the loans when they are due, the private equity lenders usually renew the loans at the current going rates, which are very often higher, and at new fees, etc. Equity lenders—especially the private ones—love that. They *wait* for a loan to come up for renewal. The seniors at that point are at their mercy. Should the lender choose not to renew the loan, the senior is then faced with a quick sale or possible foreclosure."

"What's different about you?" I asked him.

"I always make it a point to ask, 'Can you really repay this loan?' I spell it out for them, bit by bit. And I never fail to mention that other, more sensible option: why not sell your home and downgrade your lifestyle? Then you wouldn't owe anybody anything."

"How can we consumers recognize a usurious lender?" I asked Blaney.

"They'll be on a one-to-one relationship and not usually operating as licensed real estate loan brokers or state financial institutions. As licensed real estate loan brokers we are under constant scrutiny by the California State Real Estate Commissioner and we have very specific rules of what we can and cannot do. Legitimate brokers and lenders will not make usurious loans. The last thing they want is your property in foreclosure, senior or not. But if a senior's income has dropped to an unacceptable conforming loan limit, the loan will not be made. That is not to say that there are not other types of loans at higher rates, fees and at lesser loan to values that can fill the needs of some. But if you take one of those loans or go to a private/hard equity lender, have a plan of action. A legitimate real estate lender will work through a brokerage or a bank. He must be state and federally insured. He'll be constantly audited by the state's real estate board, so you can always call the real estate board in your state to see if there's ever been a complaint against him. Remember, usury is illegal, so all those businesses operating under the big state's umbrella can't just go and charge usurious interest rates. But nothing can stop a private party from charging whatever they can get, and if they are represented by a licensed agent the charge can be steep. If these private lenders are not licensed or working through a licensed agent, there are very definite limits to the rates they can charge. If you *ever* feel the rate or fees or terms are uncomfortable, call your attorney or ask the State Department of Real Estate or State Consumers Affairs folks in Sacramento. Don't let your home be taken from you through any means without questioning it thoroughly, and that may include your family, friends, and local attorney. Now, if you're in bankruptcy, a good attorney can advise you. If you have enough equity in the house, foreclosure can be stalled, the home can be sold, and you can get your equity back. So I also advise seniors to look into bankruptcy. Don't talk to just one advisor and lender, though. Talk to many.

"Yes, I feel my responsibility to these people. I need to be able to sleep at night. Frankly, this business is busy enough—too busy, in fact! God, just look at this desk—I don't need to take people's homes to get by.

"The important thing to know is that a fat return is what most lenders want. They don't really care too much about your ability to pay."

"What about culpability on the lenders' part? What do you think could be done to prevent some of these loans being given to people who can't pay?"

"I think counseling should be mandatory. Not only lending institutions, but the family or heirs of the seniors really should take an interest in their financial well-being. We counsel all ages of potential borrowers, and we are very careful when dealing with fixed-income customers (usually seniors). All lending institutions should be required to counsel potential borrowers. I've had seniors come in here who couldn't pay their nineteen-dollar heat bill. I won't give them a loan because they won't be able to pay it. Yes, counseling should be mandatory, and every couple years, too. Seniors should be asked by the lender, 'How are you doing? Making ends meet? Are you buying the medicine you need?' Yes, I think we could stop a lot of shysters if there had to be a 'counseling stamp' before any loan could be given."

"How do you feel about Joy Simmons' comment that old people are discriminated against because of their age and that no one's willing to give an old person a long-term loan because they're going to die soon, and that most lenders instead push balloon payments on old people?"

"We are scrutinized very closely by the Federal Trade Commission.

All loan applications are reviewed on a regular basis internally and by the lender and finally by the State or Feds. There had better not be an instance where anyone is discriminated against because of age, sex, religion, you name it. Tell your readers that if they feel they've been discriminated against for any of those reasons, they can call the FTC in Washington, D.C., at 1-202-724-1140."

What to Do If You Feel You Have Been Ripped Off

Always write down on your calendar the time of the year your property taxes are due. If you do not receive a statement, immediately call your county tax assessor's office or whomever handles your property tax questions. Although it's lovely to imagine, "Gee, maybe this month I don't owe them," you do. Death and taxes, as they say, are the only certainties in life, so if you don't get word, immediately look into it. Someone could have stolen your property, and they could be paying the taxes on it. If they are, they can slap all kinds of expensive loans against your property, or even boot you out! If the worst has happened and the tax assessor's office says you don't own the property anymore, get a lawyer. If you're a senior, ask your local senior center for advice, or look in the government pages of your phone book for "Senior Legal Aid" or "Area Department of Aging—Legal Aid." The social services section of your phone book's government section has a wealth of headings pertinent to you as a senior in need of legal help. As equity rip-offs occur mostly to the elderly, you'll meet with attorneys who are experienced in this matter.

If you have missed even one payment on your mortgage loan, a notice of default can be recorded at any time. You then have three months to pay the missing monthly payments; this is called "curing the default." This three-month period is called the "reinstatement period." FHA/VA regulations require a lender making a federally insured loan to take reasonable steps to counsel a homeowner whenever a default occurs. Make sure this happens, and options for you to remedy the situation are discussed.

There are three remedies for defaults:

Forbearance The lender specifies a period of time in which he will either reduce, increase, or suspend regular monthly payments. Forbearance is designed to compensate for periods of financial difficulty. Often, payments can be reduced or suspended, with the agreement that they'll be made up at some date in the future.

Recasting The lender and homeowner extend the mortgage term for an agreed-upon period of time; hence, a twenty-year mortgage might become a thirty-year mortgage after recasting. This will allow monthly payments to be reduced to a more manageable size for the homeowner.

Assignment or Refunding The homeowner stops making payments for a period of time, if the homeowner qualifies. FHA/VA will make the payments, but then the homeowner must pay them instead of the lender. There are many rules about this option, and you can look into it by calling your local FHA/VA office.

Once you get into trouble by missing a few payments, and a notice of default or trustee's sale is recorded, you can expect to be flooded with mail from all types of con artists offering to rescue you from all your problems. Beware of these! Throw those letters away immediately! People calling themselves "foreclosure counselors" or "foreclosure specialists" are really rip-off artists, and what they operate is a swindle that will take your home. They search county records and foreclosure journals every day to find names of homeowners in default. They approach their victims with "a deal you can't refuse." You can, and you must, refuse these shady deals. What all the nation's attorneys general repeat to their constituents should become your mantra: "If it sounds too good to be true, it probably is!" Go to a Legal Aid Center, or to some other professional equipped to give you sound legal facts.

If you find yourself in foreclosure, act immediately, don't wait until you become desperate. Seek professional counseling, and not the counseling from brochures or flyers from "foreclosure counselors" or "foreclosure specialists." Don't ignore any papers you receive regarding your home. Read all the papers you receive very carefully, and if you don't understand every word, have an attorney go over them.

If no crimes have been committed against you but you need assistance with your loan, various agencies to contact in your county, city, or state may have names such as Legal Services Program, Legal Aid Foundation, or the Department of Consumer Affairs listed under your county's name. There may also be a Consumer Credit Counselor in your city, or a Home Loan Counseling Center.

If you feel that a crime has been committed, one place you can contact for help is your state's Attorney General's office Crime Prevention Unit. They may direct you to your District Attorney, or your City Attorney. No matter what the crime, be sure to call the Better Business Bureau in your area. If you want to check records, a good resource is the Register Recorder's office in your area.

Telemarketing Fraud

How $40 Billion a Year Is
Fleeced From People Over Fifty-Five

THE FOLLOWING IS a transcript from a victim's recording of an actual crime committed against her. (Because the case was settled without admission of liability, I'll use fictitious names in the discussion below.) "Edna," the victim, had a hearing problem, and routinely recorded all her phone calls so she could go over them later to hear what she'd missed. The tape recording was used by the Federal Trade Commission as evidence against the telemarketing con artists involved and is public record. Prosecution of this ring of telemarketing con artists was successful, and the perpetrators are behind bars. "Fred" in this transcript is the "front man," or salesman, trying to get Edna's last stash of money.

Fred: How are you this morning?

Edna: Fine.

Fred: Great to hear it. Well, Edna, the only reason for the call today is we've just acquired some of your paperwork here at the Charity Network in Massachusetts. Your paperwork confirming that earlier last month right before Thanksgiving, you may have signed up and sent in an entry form for a sweepstakes from your home, trying to win some cash. Do you remember, Edna?

Edna: Yes.

Fred: Great…. Well, Edna, the reason for the call today is, first of all, to let you know you can relax. I'm not selling anything. I'm calling from the Charity Network because as a direct result of that entry form, without purchase necessary, you were hand-selected by the Charity Network as one of our grand national winners today. Congratulations to you, Edna.

Edna: Well, thank you.

Fred: You're very welcome. Now, before I get you excited, you did check a little box down here on the entry form and it says, 'I have never won or received a major prize or winnings in excess of $3,000 before.' Is that correct? You never won the lottery or anything worth over $3,000, Edna?

Edna: I have never won anything over twenty-five bucks, I don't think.

Fred: Oh. Okay. Then you qualify. And just so you know now, we're a charity. We run the fund-raising giveaway every year to generate publicity for us and, Edna, you'll never say 'never' again, and since you're already a winner, I want you to have a pen and a piece of paper ready when I give you the details. Okay. Now, Edna, I work for a charity. Now, the name of the charity is called Endeavor. I'm calling from the Endeavor Charity Network. And my name is Fred Hansen. And, Edna, the reason for the call is you were selected and now, by law, you must receive one of our top five premiums. Now, number one is your choice: either a brand-new Mercedes Benz, coming fully loaded. That's a brand new car, Edna. A Mercedes Benz. Have you seen what those look like? Now, since some folks wouldn't be able to afford the insurance or the registration fees, I want to let you know if you don't drive the Mercedes Benz home from your local authorized Mercedes Benz dealership, you can take the cash instead, and this year it's $50,000, Edna.

Edna: Oh, my goodness.

Fred: How does that sound?

Edna: Boy. It sounds like something that would save my life right now.

Fred: What would you do with the $50,000 for Christmas if you got it?

Edna: I would put it down on my living quarters so I can get my mortgage paid off and my payments down to where I could afford to keep my home.

Fred: Is it a condominium?

Edna: Yes, it is.

Fred: Oh, great. We just got my mom one in southern California. Now, Edna, so that your paperwork matches mine, I want you to circle the $50,000. You need the cash, right? Well, you deserve it, hon. You know, if that would help you with the condo, I would feel so good inside. Category number two, Edna, is cash also. Now, this one is $7,500. Now, Edna, because of possible redemption charges in the State of Illinois, today it's preferable, if you get the cash, that you have an active checking account or savings account with at least an active balance of $2,000. Which one applies to you?

Edna: Well, neither. I have the money in the money market.

Fred: Oh, that's smarter anyway. You do have at least $2,000 in the money market account, then?

Edna: Yes.

Fred: Now that's just because they like to get the awards out within twenty-four hours....

Fred continued in this manner, telling Edna the other categories of awards, all of which would have improved her life significantly. At one point, he said:

Fred: I want you to know that I am the national director of Endeavor Charity, and that I'm calling from the Endeavor Charity Network. You should know that Endeavor, through our feeding centers in over 190 cities in America, helps to put children, senior citizens, and women who through no fault of their own are either homeless or hungry, back into places to live. It is the goal of Endeavor to put an end to hunger and the homeless problem in America. Now, since we're registered with the IRS as a 501(c)3, a non-profit organization, and recognized as such, every year through tremendous corporate sponsors, Fortune 500 companies and small businesses, we've received some really nice gifts. And because you signed up, you're guaranteed one of those. I want to let you know, since this has already happened for you, we do ask two things of you. But I'm certainly sure both of them are going to make you feel really good about winning. First of all, Edna, we'd like to see a picture of you smiling for us after you receive the award.

Edna: No problem.

Fred: Now, secondly, with our program here in aiding and assisting homeless and needy Americans, we also ask for a small donation which is tax-deductible, and which will allow us to show that, because you care about fellow Americans in need, you got the big award, and that will ultimately increase our donations nationwide from corporations and from individuals like yourself. Endeavor Charity Network has three levels for donations, and you get to choose the one that's best for you. Do you own your own business, Edna?

Edna: No. The fact is, I'm a widow, and...well...because of a health problem I wasn't able to work anymore, and so I'm just hanging on by the skin of my teeth wondering where my next, where, what's it going to come from when I get done with my, the disability, the...I think I probably qualify for your charity more than I would your prizes.

Fred heard Edna tell him her desperate economic situation, yet *there are nine more pages in this transcript!* Fred continued to badger Edna with things such as "Now, Edna, you don't want the people of America to think you don't care about the homeless, do you?" The lowest level of donation amount—the "Bronze Level"—was $1,100, but Edna said she couldn't manage even that. Fred told her, with great compassion, that because he understood her financial situation, he would right now speak to his supervisor and allow her to pay the "super senior discount for just $880 even." He gave her the address in Massachusetts where she should send the money, and she said she would.

Edna wrote the check for $880 and sent it FedEx as instructed, but then had second thoughts. She cancelled the check, called the authorities, and the Federal Trade Commission tracked down "Fred" and his boiler room. The tape was made in a state in which only "one-party consent" is necessary for phone conversations to be taped legally. Thus, it was permissible for the tape to be used as evidence in federal court.

The importance of one woman taping this conversation cannot be overestimated; the Federal Trade Commission had been working to crack a huge interstate ring, and Edna's work helped them connect the final links in the case. This case led to the successful conclusion on the part of the plaintiffs in a class-action suit. The defendants included ten individuals and nine different corporations, all of which practiced telemarketing fraud. The group of corporations had been fleecing primarily elderly victims from boiler rooms in Louisiana, Massachusetts, Nevada, and California.

Aggressive and Sharp:
Margaret Stanish, Deputy Attorney General,
Consumer and Telemarketing Fraud Unit,
Las Vegas, Nevada

One of the most ferocious warriors in America tackling the crime of telemarketing fraud is Margaret Stanish. She is the Deputy Attorney General of Nevada, and works out of Las Vegas—the telemarketing fraud boiler room capital of America. She has her own Telemarketing and Consumer Fraud Unit.

I visited Stanish in Las Vegas just after she'd busted a deplorable group of con artists. While trying to work me into her busy schedule, she told me that on the day I'd picked to meet her in Las Vegas, she'd be in court for the sentencing of the leader of an interstate telemarketing fraud ring. He had begun his dirty work in Florida—another large mecca for boiler room operators—and Stanish currently had him in prison without bail. I asked her for the details. She told me that he had started in Florida. He had a printout of all the people—mostly seniors in Florida—who had purchased timeshares. He'd call and say, "We've located a buyer for your timeshare!" Most people were thrilled by the high prices these so-called buyers were willing to pay, and had no problem when he said, "Now, just send one thousand dollars to cover all the paperwork for the property transfer costs, and we'll send you all your money!" They sent those thousand-dollar checks and, of course, never heard from him again. In four weeks in Florida he made $2 million. Then he moved his operation to Las Vegas, and in another four weeks he'd made $200,000.

I asked Stanish what major changes she had seen in the types of telemarketing fraud occurring? She replied that Nevada was well established as a telemarketing haven back in the days of the so-called "money for a prize" scams. Then, in 1989, 599.B was passed to try to combat that kind of fraud. The con artists would tell their marks that they had won this great prize, and now all they needed to do was send in money ($4 to $1,000) to pick up their prizes. They always said the amount was less than the prize they'd won, which was never true.

In 1991, the Federal Trade Commission filed several lawsuits against all these Nevada telemarketing operations, and that eliminated that kind of fraud. Stanish said that mostly what she sees now is

telefunding types of fraud, such as the one Edna taped of the Endeavor Charity. By representing non-profit organizations, con artists
can escape regulations. The Supreme Court, under the First Amendment, has ruled that charitable speech is protected from regulation.

In addition, telemarketing con artists sometimes work within
other, perfectly legal means. As examples, Stanish described how telemarketing con artists go to smaller charities desperate for funds—like
the Endeavor Charity Network—and offer them money they can't
refuse. The con artists only give 5% of their total take to the charity
organization, but that's 5% they wouldn't get otherwise. The con artists then offer a potentially huge prize, saying, "Make a donation and
get your big prize and a tax deduction." But when the consumer sees
the actual prize, it's garbage (Stanish showed me the prizes, and they
truly were junk) but the consumer feels good anyway, because he or
she has given to charity. They don't complain too much, Stanish said.

I then asked Stanish how many complaints she received, and she
said about 1,000 a month on telemarketing fraud. Some of them
come from the con artists themselves, and involve a type of fraud
known as "recovery services scam." In this type of scam, the con artists
buy a list of consumers who have been had by other telemarketing
con artists. The salesmen of all the boiler rooms in the country work
together to compile these lists. Then the supposed recovery service
calls the consumer and says, "We know you were ripped off, so we
want to work with you to try to get your money back. If you'll just pay
$600 to cover legal fees, we'll get that money back for you." And, of
course, that $600 is just as gone as the original money. There's no way
a recovery service could get the money from the original boiler room,
because often it's been out of business for years, and the owner is
locked in jail.

Stanish also told me that telemarketing fraud attracts transients.
Salespeople go off on their own and start their own boiler rooms. For
example, they'll start a Western Union scam. Armed with a list of previous victims—perhaps the ones they themselves have ripped off—
they call and say, "Remember that contest you entered?" They know
which contest these consumers have entered in the last year. "You actually won that Cadillac!" they shout. "Just send $2,000 to cover regis-
tration and licensing fees and send it to Western Union. Make the
check out to [whatever phoney business name or fake I.D. name

they're using]." Western Union is all over the world, so it's almost impossible to track down such scams. Stanish said that scams like this are her current big headache.

But Stanish did catch one of these, with the help of a victim, and the con artist is now in jail awaiting his sentencing hearing. The victim was a man who lived in Alaska. He'd previously purchased vitamins through a telemarketer, so he was on the con artist's computer list. The con artist informed him that when he purchased those vitamins—and the con artist knew exactly which vitamins, because it was on the card—he had automatically entered a promotion contest. He informed the man that he'd won big, of course. The victim had been burned before by telemarketing con artists, so he was mad. He taped his whole conversation with this con artist, who gave him a Nevada address and phone number. The victim in Alaska then called Stanish, and her office did a sting operation. They had the victim call the boiler room back and tell them he was too far from a Western Union office (the con artists had of course told him to send the money via Western Union) and asked if he could send the money Federal Express? The con artists said yes, and Stanish's office got them.

In that particular case, another of the con artists' victims testified on the stand. She was a retired school teacher, Stanish said, and a really bright woman. So much for the misconception that only dumb people get taken! Stanish said she had even worked with a judge who had been ripped off. This teacher's testimony was powerful. She was furious at what had been done to her, and was a great witness. But Stanish also said that some of her victims have been taken by so many different scams that they're confused and don't make good witnesses.

Asked why she thinks Las Vegas is the boiler room capital of America, Stanish said that a Las Vegas address is a hook. People think there's a better chance in Las Vegas of winning something for nothing. Las Vegas boiler rooms are more successful, she said. She's even had Massachusetts and New York boiler rooms using Las Vegas addresses and bank accounts.

Partly for this reason, Nevada is one of the only states in the U.S. that has its own telemarketing and consumer fraud unit. In Stanish's unit there are four attorneys, three investigators, and one paralegal. But, of course, for interstate crimes they work very closely with the Federal Trade Commission, the FBI, the U.S. Postal Inspector, and others. And they've been successful. Due to some really hard work, in one year the number of fraudulent telemarketing companies operating in Nevada went from eighty down to forty-two. That's quite a change in the landscape of the crime!

Since 1993, Stanish said, they mostly just have the telefunders, who use people's good hearts to get their money. They always use the "charity du jour"—after an earthquake, they're collecting for earthquake victims; AIDS babies are currently very popular. People want to make the world better, but instead all their money's going into a boiler room. Stanish likes to quote from "Star Trek": "Our enemies cloaked in good deeds are the most difficult to detect." It's true.

According to Stanish, the crime occurs when con artists misrepresent themselves. With the recovery service scam, for example, the con artists say they're affiliated with the government or some law firm, or that it's even possible to get one dime back from a company that's long out of business. That's illegal.

Finally, I asked Stanish what change she would most like to see in the way these criminals are dealt with? Without hesitation she said she'd like to see them pay restitution to the victims. Judges want to save our limited jail space for violent criminals, and that can be hard for prosecutors to accept after they've worked so hard to gather evidence. Restitution, therefore, is Stanish's next big goal.

Nationwide Response to Telemarketing Fraud

Margaret Stanish left me in front of a VCR/TV so I could watch some video tapes she'd made on telemarketing fraud in America. The opening segment, produced by the Securities Division of the Secretary of State in Nevada, showed Betty White telling Nevadans that in America, "One million dollars every hour is robbed by criminals using phones." The segment that followed was from the television program "A Current Affair" and its segment "The Gotcha! Files," in which reporters go undercover. In this segment, the reporter went undercover to work in a Buffalo, New York, boiler room to expose telemarketing fraud. The company, headquartered in Las Vegas, was making $30 million a year before it was closed down.

"Boiler room" is such a great name for these phone operations, because that's what they sound like! There are many, many people on the phones calling from tiny cubicles. One front man on the video tape was trying to convince someone that he had won a car and that if he used his credit card to buy something, he'd get the car.

According to Thomas J. Coyle, an FBI agent interviewed on the same program, "Ninety-two percent of homes in the United States have been contacted by a telemarketing con-artist operation." He went on to say that, "Credit cards are the fastest way for the companies to get money into their Las Vegas-based bank accounts. And every year credit card companies estimate they lose about $300 million due to credit card fraud."

One victim, a woman, was "so embarrassed!" In one day, telemarketers got her for $13,000. For this money, she got a few cleaning and beauty products.

Salespeople are offered very good money for conning victims— about $5,000 a week. That will buy a lot of conscience, but on the tape one salesman admitted to his friend that he felt "real bad, ripping off all these old people." His friend—also a con-artist telephone salesman—told his buddy, "You gotta do it. You're making good money."

The next segment showed a salesman doing his phone pitch, saying, "You are guaranteed by law to walk away with a big prize."

So what is being done about this scourge? Lawmakers have begun to act. In August, 1994, law number PL103-297, entitled "Telemarketing and Consumer Fraud and Abuse Prevention Act" (H.R. 868) became effective. This law gives more interstate power to the Federal Trade Commission and to attorneys general to interact with other interstate and federal agencies in arresting and sentencing con artists. It forbids telemarketers to phone the same consumer repeatedly, calling this pattern "coercive or abusive of the customer's right to privacy," it restricts times of day when telemarketers may phone, and it stipulates that "...any telephone solicitor shall promptly and clearly disclose the purpose of the call." The bill also gives attorneys general the power to bring civil suits against illegal telemarketing operations in order to bring financial restitution to the victims, and it gives the same power to citizens who have lost more that $50,000: you can sue the tails off these con artists.

In a September 1994 hearing on Capitol Hill, William J. Esposito, Deputy Assistant Director of the FBI, testified before Congress on the need for even further action to stop telemarketing fraud. He began by pointing out that legitimate telemarketing companies generate $400 billion annually and employ over 3.4 million people. We can assume, he intimated, that telemarketing is here to stay. But fraud is costing consumers one tenth of that, or $40 billion annually, and that must end. An in-depth study conducted by the FBI confirmed that the elderly are the primary targets of unscrupulous telemarketing con artists, with the distant runner-up being owners of very small businesses.

In the Senate the bill was strongly supported by Senator Bryan of Nevada and Senator John McCain of Arizona. During Senator Bryan's testimony, he cited the Consumer Federation of America and the National Association of Consumer Agency Administrators. When they asked state and local consumer protection agencies, "What is the worst consumer rip-off and abuse you see?", the unanimous response was, "Telemarketing fraud." Furthering Mr. Esposito's figures that 92% of American households have been approached by telemarketing con artists via the mail or the telephone, Senator Bryan quoted figures from the National Consumers League indicating that 29% of those approached had responded. Five and a half million people last year complained they had bought via telephone something that "they now feel was a definite fraud...items are either never delivered, or are not of the value which the consumer was promised."

Meanwhile, Iowa's attorney general has virtually stopped telemarketing scams in her state. Beginning in November of 1994, Bonnie Campbell, Attorney General of Iowa, sent out warning packets to explain Iowa's novel undercover sting operation against telemarketing con artists. Basically, the sting took the phone numbers of Iowans who have been victimized by con artists—and, hence, who are on all the con artists' lists as "easy marks"—and reassigned them to ring directly into the attorney general's office. The con artists then did their spiels, not knowing to whom they were speaking, and the entire conversation was taped. The former victims were given new telephone numbers, and probably have learned to "just say no" or slam the phone when a con artist calls. The attorney general can prosecute more easily with the incriminating tapes.

In one month after this program was initiated in Iowa, 400 telemarketing con artists' conversations were taped. Civil and criminal actions have begun in earnest against the con artists. This is great news for consumers across the country, as telemarketing scams are never confined within one state's borders. In fact, most of the complaints made by Iowa consumers were focused on telemarketers in Las Vegas. Ms. Campbell, therefore, says that most of her warning packets are being sent to Las Vegas telemarketing operations. In the packet is a flier that warns: "Telemarketers: If your sales practices violate Iowa laws, and if you do not want to risk having your pitches taped by the Attorney General of Iowa, please post this notice in your telephone room. Do not call Iowa!"

I urge all of you to contact your own state Attorney General and request that a similar program be implemented in your state. Ask what you can do to help get it going. Also, please read the chapter on "Preventing Telemarketing Rip-offs," as it lists a variety of free pamphlets you can request that will enlighten you. Mail- and telephone-order companies who provide legitimate products and services are lifesavers for those of you who don't get out and about as easily as you once did. That is why the mail-order business is doing so well. But we must all be more savvy about buying through the mail and over the phone.

An Honest Telemarketer: Interview with an Angry Anti-Fraud Lobbyist

Steve Sisolak lives in Las Vegas and runs American Distributing Company, a legitimate firm that sells custom imprinted advertising items to businesses: pens imprinted with a local beauty salon's name and number, for example. As he really can't afford to send salesmen out on the road selling these things, he depends on the telephone and catalog sales. Sisolak became a lobbyist, lobbying for tougher legislation against telemarketing fraud. He wanted to see Nevada Deputy Attorney General Margaret Stanish's office get better funding so that she could put more con artists behind bars. It was fascinating for me to hear about telemarketing fraud from Sisolak's perspective and to hear it was destroying his business. His feelings about fraud were understandably passionate, and they're worth reading.

"I'm not convinced," Sisolak said, "that lawmakers want to make the hard decisions. Larger magazine companies have employed lobbyists who are big campaign contributors. They were successful in getting forty-two loopholes!"

"But you were successful, both in getting Margaret's office some funding and in getting some tougher legislation."

"Yes, we were successful in enhancing penalties when seniors are targeted in telemarketing scams. Triple damages when perpetrators target seniors. Nevada State Senator Dina Titus sponsored that bill just last session. But you can't legislate moral values. Laws are no good without the funding to enforce them. This is the problem in Nevada. The fact that the laws exist make people complacent. I'm saying, if you work at Western Union and an elderly person is wiring $5,000 somewhere, you have a moral obligation to stop the transaction if you know it's a rip-off.

"And MasterCard and Visa. They know in one day when a company is doing something wrong. Valley Bank in Las Vegas knew, and they had the guts to say, 'no more telemarketing accounts allowed in this bank!' Even me, and I'm legit. But I respect them. Other banks around here that manage the credit card accounts are making $2-$3 million a *week* on fraud operations. They suffer no consequences, so they're not doing a thing to stop it. No, I think if they wanted to stop the problem, they could."

We talked some more about the culpability of banks, as it has turned up as a solution in many kinds of elder financial abuse—from abuse by family relatives to home equity fraud—and Sisolak agreed. "Make them culpable in this instance, too."

"Give me an example of how illegal telemarketers are hurting you—besides, of course, getting your bank account closed."

"Here in Las Vegas, there are newspaper ads all the time offering $3,000-$5,000 a week to be a telephone salesperson in an illegal boiler room. [No, the ads don't say that, they just offer the big paycheck.] My firm pays phone salespeople $300-$400 a week. I can't get anyone to work for me! I've been using telemarketing for twenty years, and now every day my partner and I question whether we can go on.

"See, we're into the fifth generation of telemarketing fraud, and these twenty-year-old salespeople are driving around in Jaguars. They *idolize* the owners of fraudulent telemarketing companies and they think they're all above the law. We're talking about a crime that takes $100,000, $200,000—some people's entire life savings! I've heard the testimony of these victims. It'll tear your heart out, listening to them. I see this as an enforcement problem. There is no consequence for the people committing these crimes, and I can't understand it. To me there is no difference between putting a gun to an elderly woman's head and taking her life's savings, and taking it this way. But these con artists don't ever do time. And why does it take so long [up to five years just to gather evidence] to prosecute people? This is sending the wrong message.

"Most of the people you try to educate will say, 'Oh, I would never fall for that!' But they do."

"I've heard that you've been to the legislature to testify."

"Yes, and on the criminal ladder, this crime ranks pretty low. People getting caught shoplifting to feed their families get treated more harshly than people stealing the entire life savings of a bunch of old people."

"You've been very active trying to get MasterCard and Visa to accept some culpability. Could you go into that?"

"MasterCard and Visa know who the telemarketing con artists are. Any business that sends in unsigned drafts is either mail order or a telemarketer. When you have a telemarketer who is getting 15% charge backs—that's where you submit an affidavit and merchants have to reverse those charges—come on! Visa knows there's a problem when 20% of a company's customers are unhappy! But they allow it. At 15% charge back, a red flag should go up. They should take away a telemarketer's merchant account, or face culpability charges down the line. At the very least they should look into it, say, 'Excuse me, but 20% of your customers have a problem. What are you doing?' But now there's nothing.

"Some of these telemarketing fraud accounts in Las Vegas have $2–$3 million on deposit as a kind of credit limit—what they're allowed to charge in a month. Five million dollars is the largest account I know of in Las Vegas. So the bank's getting $5 million to use, money just sitting there for the bank. The banks should be prosecuted along with all the guys stealing elderly people's life savings. And if there were more people like Deputy Attorney General Margaret Stanish, we could take care of the problem.

"The U.S. Postal Service was so big and so effective prosecuting mail fraud that the mail fraud people went to telephones and private companies like Western Union, FedEx, and UPS. Now there's a new group of people ripping off the elderly. They have no fear because they've never seen their associates lose all their money and go to prison. That's how you stop the situation. They know nothing's going to happen to them. They know it's wrong, but there's no consequence. If the consequence doesn't come for five years, it doesn't do any good. There is no difference between what they're doing and kicking in the door and robbing these elderly people at gunpoint. Now there's the charity fraud, where the victims thought they were really helping the most desperate people in the world.

"I know people who do this charity telemarketing fraud."

"The salespeople and front men?"

"Sure, because in Las Vegas there are so many of them, you can't help but know a few. They know it's wrong, but they're making from $3,000 up to $10,000 a week, so they say to me, 'If I don't do it, somebody else will.' Hey, you can make 10K just on one phone call! I say prosecute everyone when you shut down an illegal room: the secretaries, front people, everyone. These companies are making up to $30 million a year on very little overhead. I want harsh measures to keep the phone as a legitimate tool for me and the other honest people who want to work for a living.

"Right now, the people who have worked to stop telemarketing fraud have made a difference. Margaret Stanish is one of them. Telemarketers avoid her like the plague. There are also four states the con artists don't call these days: Iowa, Idaho, Oregon, and, now, Nevada. California could have been another. They were very close when the FTC did three or four big sting operations. Those were civil cases, but if they'd also brought criminal actions, California wouldn't have the fraud problem they have. I mean, the companies made $10 million. So what if they have to spend two on a civil case? Nobody went to jail. Only the victims ate it. Do I sound heated up enough about all this for you?"

"You do."

Operation Disconnect:
An FBI Assault on Boiler Rooms

Operation Disconnect was a massive sting operation by the FBI in which 123 illegal boiler rooms were identified. Seventy-nine locations all across America were searched, and 540 subjects were arrested. There were boiler rooms in Washington, D.C., Baltimore, Phoenix, New Orleans, Houston, Tampa, Miami, Dallas, Detroit, Atlanta, Chicago, Las Vegas, Jacksonville, San Diego, Los Angeles, and other cities. The origin of Operation Disconnect was in an illegal boiler room in Salt Lake City. Among the glories of this sting's success is that the prison sentences imposed on the con artists are the longest yet for white-collar crime in America. I spoke with Keith DeVincentis, who arrives at his desk at seven a.m. each morning. Keith is a Supervisory Special Agent in the FBI's Economic Crimes Squad in San Diego, California. He said he would walk me through Operation Disconnect and its importance in stopping telemarketing fraud.

"Keith, I wanted to first ask you about the victims, because during this massive sting the FBI concentrated a lot on victim profiles."

"Yes, and elderly widows are definitely the main targets. They're the easiest to sell to, and the easiest to reload. And recovery rooms target elderly widows almost exclusively."

("Reload" means to sell to again and again, and "recovery rooms" are scam operations in which a victim who's already been ripped off is told that a "recovery service" will get the money back for her if she'll pay attorney fees, etc.)

"How many calls do you get in this FBI office on telemarketing fraud?"

"Several hundred calls a month. That's just the calls I personally get. Many people are embarrassed to complain. The boiler room has taken the elderly person's last shred of dignity. It can cause big problems in the family. Adult children will often put their parents into conservatorship because of this, because they think their parents have become incapacitated. But the guys working the phones get people under ether—so people don't even know they're being defrauded. A lot of times, relatives or law enforcement officers call the FBI. Hundreds of thousands of dollars can be taken."

"In Operation Disconnect were those 540 subjects just the owners of the boiler rooms, or were they also the phone salespeople?"

"Owners, fronters, and reloaders. Fronters are the new callers who set up the first sale. They are the cog of the wheel. Reloaders generate most of the money."

"Were you able to seize money?"

"We seized $4.5 million in cash, boats, cars, and weapons."

"Any convictions yet?"

"As of December '94, 114 people have been convicted just in San Diego, and nationwide we're also doing great."

"What kind of sentences are they getting?"

"Typically, white-collar crime is short. But for example, defendants in the Amtel 'Say No to Drugs' operation [in which victims spend a fortune for Just Say No kits—a lot of cheap junk] received 120 and 108 months in jail [ten years and nine years, respectively]. Five years is the smallest sentence any of the Operation Disconnect subjects have received, so judges do realize how devastating this crime is. Also, under the new sentencing guidelines there is enhancement of time for the vulnerability of the victims."

"How long did Operation Disconnect take?"

"It began in Salt Lake City in 1990, and offices were seized three years later."

"Can you tell me how your agents were able to get in?"

"Our objective was to get tape-recorded conversations of the con artists saying exactly what they were doing. So our pitch was, 'We have an automatic dialing machine that will dial a whole bunch of phones and pre-identify victims with questions like "How old are you?" The appeal was enormous. Their problems are huge phone bills. The machine made 24,000 phone calls in an hour. The victims call you back with this system, and they were already identified. The FBI asked for a percentage of the con artists' profit, and in this way we could get a picture of the amount of money involved.

"Then agents with telephones called in as victims. The phone calls were taped. The FBI went to the grand jury with all this easy evidence, and we got 'Probable Cause to Search.'"

"Were you able to get any money back to the victims?"

"Not much. To individual victims, no. That's almost impossible. Boiler room operators tend to be drug-addicted, alcoholic, spendthrifts. No, if you give your money to these guys, it's gone. Cars, coke, clothes. FBI agents are always shocked at how these people can spend so much money. Often there are 20,000 or 30,000 victims. Even after the sale of the seized assets, how do you go about recovery? In just one boiler room in San Diego there were 20,000 victims."

"I don't suppose you know how many victims there were nation-wide?"

"Staggering. Probably millions. It's unknowable."

"Tell me about the day you stormed the boiler rooms."

"National Take Down Day was March 4, 1993. An average of 200 agents in each of eighteen cities across America were on the streets storming boiler rooms. This is what the FBI does best."

"Who initiates such an operation?"

"When telemarketing con artists pick up the phone, they violate the 'Liars Statute.' If they make interstate calls, it's our jurisdiction. We have a task force that meets quarterly. The Federal Trade Commission shares information. They are a major source. There has to be an interstate law violated for the FBI to get involved."

"When I spoke with Steve Sisolak, he said front runners don't get punished."

"I hate to disagree with anyone, but that's no longer true. Many front runners in Operation Disconnect were punished. I think laws do include front room salesmen. But I also think the judiciary should be better educated on these laws. I think it's changing for the better. In Operation Disconnect we exploded salesmen's claims. Their defense was 'We didn't know the prizes were crummy, or that it was a rip-off.' Everybody knows everything, and our tapes proved it. Things will change. The penalties are available, and adequate if applied. More front room salespeople will be convicted. It's only a matter of time. The precedents have been set. For reloaders in Operation Disconnect, the average jail time was seventy-eight to eighty months in prison [six and a half years]."

"What is your advice to the public?"

"When you're solicited by phone, just hang up. These guys are skilled professional cheats. To lonely widows they are extraordinarily charming. They'll send you birthday cards and Christmas ornaments. Don't become involved, because they're too good.

"If you have been victimized, you must report it. Do not be ashamed or embarrassed to report. We don't know they're out there until you call. We could get one complaint about a boiler room that has thousands of victims. We don't judge you, so don't be embarrassed. Call the FBI or your state's Attorney General."

Preventing Telemarketing Rip-Offs: What To Do If You Get Hit by Con Artists

The rotten truth is, the day you turn fifty-five, or the day your spouse dies, the con artists put you on their calling list. You will be contacted. My mother is a widow, and she receives about twenty unsolicited phone calls a day, most of them between the hours of four and six p.m.

As she says, "If someone asks for Mrs. Harriett Brown, now, that's not the way my friends or family address me. They say, 'Mom,' or 'Grandma,' or 'Harriett.' So if I hear 'Mrs. Harriett Brown,' I say, 'No, she's not in right now, may I take a message?' and if they leave a message I care about, I'll get back to them. But solicitors never leave a message. They always say, 'Oh, I'll call back later.' A lot of them still ask for Vern [her late husband], and when they do, I just hang up. He's been gone twelve years, after all."

Taking a message is a good idea, because the "just hang up" strategy is imperfect for many of the seniors I've talked to. They always wonder if the call concerned their friends or family. This way, on the outside chance the caller is not a solicitor, he will happily leave a message.

Buying books, clothes, and household products from mail-order catalogs has to be the world's most convenient way to shop. Especially if you aren't comfortable driving in traffic or if you have a handicap, the mail, telephone, and UPS can bring the world to your doorstep. Because of all the fraud, however, you take a risk every time you use the mail or telephone to shop. Before you become a confirmed mail-and-telephone shopper, you might want to avail yourself of some of the free pamphlets mentioned below.

If you have a Visa credit card, look on your monthly statement for the number of their toll-free fraud hotline. By calling this number, you will get valuable tips on how to identify a scam and what to do if you have been victimized. Visa also offers a free brochure, "Credit

Cards: An Owner's Manual," which you can obtain either through Visa or through your local Better Business Bureau.

The Direct Marketing Association is a national trade organization representing over 3,000 companies that market products through the mail, electronic and print media, and through telemarketing. As with Steve Sisolak, telemarketing fraud hurts their business, so they work aggressively to stop it. One of their free pamphlets is "Tips on Telephone Shopping." Another is "Make Knowledge Your Partner in Mail Order Shopping." You can call the Direct Marketing Association at their offices in New York or Washington, D.C. to order these booklets free.

If you've had it with all the catalogs you're getting in the mail—or with all the phone solicitations—you can also write to the following DMA addresses to get your name taken off the lists:

Mail Preference Service
P.O. Box 3861, New York, NY, 10163

Telephone Preference Service
6 East 43rd Street, New York, NY, 10017.

Your local U.S. Postal Inspector has a booklet recently completed to educate consumers about sweepstakes, contest, and prize promotions. It's so new that at this writing there is no title, but ask about it. It does exist.

Regarding charities, the National Charities Information Bureau and the Better Business Bureau's Philanthropic Advisory Service can tell you more about charities than perhaps any other resources. The BBB's Philanthropic Advisory Service's address and phone:

Better Business Bureau's Philanthropic Advisory Service
4200 Wilson Boulevard, Arlington, VA, 22230-1804
Phone: (703)-276-0100

They can tell you about a particular national charity's activities, finances, and fundraising practices. Forty-two states are registered with them, and charities must comply; for example, a charity must donate a certain percentage of all donations received, and BBB knows the amounts, and who does and who doesn't contribute. If you've been called by a telefunder calling to get money for a charity, you should hang up; but before you hang up, you can tell them you'll be calling the BBB about their charity—just to shake them up.

Another invaluable free resource about all of this is the "Consumers' Resource Handbook." Write to: Handbook, Consumer Information Center, Pueblo, CO, 81009.

Now, if all this information has reached you too late and you feel you have been ripped off by telemarketing fraud, call the Consumer Fraud Department of the state in which the telemarketing company is based. Also call the Attorney General in your home state.

Margaret Stanish and Keith DeVincentis say they get lots of calls from adult children of victims who have been hit many times. If you are concerned about your parents, change their phone number and instruct them to hang up on solicitors. Perhaps your parents would like to become involved in a sting operation; my experience with law enforcement in general is that elders enjoy sting operations. Victims can volunteer to help "sting" a criminal, and perhaps a civil suit could be filed afterwards.

The bottom line with telephone solicitors, however, is "just say no." Hang up!

The Psychology of a Con Artist

Portrait of a Sociopath

DON IS ONE OF THE jolliest men I've ever met. He is maybe fifty-five years old and will someday be approached with a job offer to play Santa Claus for a children's charity organization. He will gladly accept, without pay, and will not quit until every child in the place is delighted. For now though, his hair is not quite gray, and his round belly is not quite huge. His goatee beard points toward the sky when he laughs, and his eyes twinkle constantly. He is one of the kindest men I have ever met, and his wife is even nicer. When they agreed to talk to me about their good buddy who took every penny of their savings, they begged me to make sure they remained anonymous, because they would feel terrible if the con artist who took their money ever found out about this. "It would really hurt his feelings if he knew we were saying bad things about him," Don's wife, Maggie, warned me.

Don had known "Jeff" (not his real name) for many years, and had watched Jeff's lifestyle grow more and more opulent. "He spent on credit cards as if he were going to die tomorrow," Don laughed. "No one would take a check from him. They all bounced. Even the credit cards—he'd go to use a card to pay for something, and the woman at the cash register would take the card away. It never mattered. He'd just go and get new cards."

Jeff seemed to really like Don and would hire Don occasionally to do work on one or another of his real estate properties. (Don is a handyman.) "I'm an easygoing guy," Don said (a gross understatement), "and I'd do the work for Jeff. He'd pay part of the money, then owe me part. I don't think he ever once paid me everything he owed me in one shot, but he'd take Maggie and me out for a nice dinner, or take us out on his boat. We had good times, and I'd get the feeling he was almost caught up with me, pay-wise. But it got out of hand. So one day I said, 'Jeff, you gotta pay me. I've got bills, and you owe me a lot.' About five grand, which for me is one hell of a lot.

"Jeff told me it was my lucky day that I could use the five thousand dollars he owed me, along with ten thousand dollars of my own, and get in on the deal of the century. I mean, he made it sound so good, he made it sound as if only a complete idiot would pass up a deal like this. That was his way. If you expressed any doubt at all, he'd sneer at you like you were retarded. For fifteen thousand dollars, he said, I could own shares in the hottest new global industry." Don broke his sentence and started laughing. "He really talked like that. And the thing was, I'd heard him sucker people before with his spiels. I was kind of a friend—an insider. I'd been with him when he'd laughed about how easy it was to sucker people. But what you've got to understand is how good people like him are at playing the con game. You've got to understand how lovable he is, how good he looks, and how well he talks. The president of MIT couldn't win against a guy like Jeff! I'm kicking myself now because I gave him everything I had, and I know it never went into any investment. I know that in my gut, even though when Jeff came to me in tears and told me the investment had gone belly-up I hugged him and comforted him. Can you imagine that? He hadn't lost a dime of his own, only other people's money, and there I was bawling for him! I knew it was all crap—there was no 'investment'—because I watched him and Candy, his knockout wife, spend the money as if they were gonna die tomorrow. I watched them do it, and now all I can do is kick myself. I have only myself to blame, I don't even blame them, and if I mentioned it to them they'd be shocked. I don't even think they realize that taking their friends' money and spending it is wrong." He laughed. "Hell, I even got an invitation from them to go to their son's wedding."

"Will you go?" I asked.

"Sure I will! It'll be the splashiest wedding of the century, and my life savings are helping to finance the affair. I wouldn't miss it, and Maggie and I will try our damndest to eat and drink about fifteen thousand dollars' worth."

When Don laughed his whole belly shook, and I believed that he and Maggie would try to have a fifteen-thousand dollar good time. It is hard for me to hear stories such as these. It is hard not to get upset. "Jeff" will go absolutely unpunished; he will continue his lavish lifestyle and will pay his expensive lawyers any time one of his victims—usually an ex-friend—tries to recoup losses. When I start to feel terrible about Don and Maggie, who are so kind, I can only comfort myself with the knowledge that they are young enough to work for another twenty years. Many victims of con artists such as Jeff and "Candy" (not her real name) are too old to earn more in the workplace. Don and Maggie have each other, and they are wiser. They promise me they'll never be suckered again, and they're such hard working people that I know they'll be able to build another nest egg somehow. They'll be okay.

A Composite Profile from Law Enforcement

I am in the bunco unit of a police station in a strange city. The detective I'm speaking with says he needs to remain anonymous because he does a lot of undercover work. As I'm listening to him, though, I'm thinking, "God, are we taxpayers getting a good deal for the money with this guy. He is so dedicated!" Today should be his day off, but he snuck into his office without telling anyone so that he could catch up on his paperwork.

He deals with "tons of guys" like Jeff, he says after I tell him about Don and Maggie's experience. "Oh, yeah, the con artists are good. They're so good!" he laughs. "Like this one con artist I brought in. This guy had been in a dozen times before, and I'd done all the investigative work on him. I had piles and piles of files on him, you follow me? I had mug shots. I'd seen him a dozen times." The detective leaned closer to me while he slammed his index finger into the table. "Do you know, when he was in front of me, and started talking a mile a minute, he was so good, I started feeling sorry for him? I started wondering if I had the right guy!" He pauses, waiting for that astonishing information to sink in, which it does. "That's how good they are."

I leave him feeling very rattled, and very vulnerable.

When I spoke to Lea Pearson, Assistant Director of the Criminal Jus-

tice Department of the AARP, she said she didn't believe statistics on
financial exploitation of the elderly, "because the victims are ashamed.
They're ashamed of themselves, and they think because they were so
stupid, they deserved to be taken. They don't report."

If I can change nothing else, I hope the above testimonies of intelligent, experienced adults change the idea that only dumb people get
conned. In all of the above cases, the men facing the con artists were
already suspicious, yet they were still seduced by them. Two of the
men make their living investigating and arresting con artists, yet even
they were fooled. In my research I have learned that those who investigate and arrest con artists may despise the con artists for what they
do, but they have a very healthy respect for the talent of sociopathic
con artists.

Dinner with Two Con Artists

I went through a great deal of red tape to visit one con artist in jail,
only to learn that he was out on parole after serving only one of the
three years he had been sentenced to serve. I couldn't believe it! He
had forged, frauded, and stolen over a million and a half dollars from
an elderly woman. I really wanted to talk to this guy, however, so I
looked him up in the white pages of his town. From working with the
undercover detective who had nailed him, I already knew where he
lived and what his spiel was. I'd been told his wife often set up meetings between her husband and prospective clients, so I called her.

On the pretext of being interested in a securities scam he was currently running—my detective friend had told me about it—I invited
him and his family to dinner. His wife, he said, would be out of town.
I didn't believe it; I firmly believed he wanted to seduce me and my
money. I hadn't mentioned that I was married or that my husband
would be present. I wanted to see how hard it would be to resist someone I knew had gone to jail for ruthlessly charming and robbing an
older woman.

First of all, the con artist and his son were extremely beautiful.
The senior con artist—I'll call him "Juan the con"—was a tall, silver-
haired, blue-eyed hunk. If I weren't already married to a handsome
man, I might have been seriously tempted by his looks alone. His son

was a younger version of Juan, with red-blond hair, a body by Soloflex, and searing, blue eyes. "Kidd" is what I'll call him.

Before their exquisitely tailored coats had dropped gracefully from their slim, perfect bodies, they were already telling me how beautiful my eyes and smile and house were, and how beautiful my children were. As a joke—well, I thought it was funny—when my husband entered I offered, "and I'm sure you'll think my husband's beautiful, too!" I'd been right, they hadn't suspected I was married. Clearly irritated, but not at all defeated, they sat down for dinner.

Their dinner conversation at first revolved around their successes. Hoping to appear knowledgeable, I told them my various theories on where the stock market was headed. They sneered at me. Their attitude seemed to be, "You aren't worth spit without our masterful guidance." I smiled and kept silent while they told us of the millions and millions of dollars' worth of deals they had closed in the last year. I could not resist blurting out, "Excuse me, Juan, how did you close all those deals? I thought you were in jail all of last year."

Juan didn't miss a beat. He slapped Kidd on the back. "My son here can handle things every bit as well as I can. They didn't have anything on me, anyway. I should never have spent one minute in the pen. I was earning an honest buck, and they knew it. It was all a setup, some idiot trying to look clean. Nobody's clean, but I was their fall guy." This is a typical con artist's attitude. (See the description of a sociopathic personality that follows excerpted from the American Psychiatric Association's *Psychiatric Glossary*.)

"Incidentally, Pamela, do you know you have the most beautiful eyes I've ever seen? Mike, I hope you don't mind my saying so. You're a very smart man."

I swear to God, he really said it just like that. I was reminded of the time when I was thirteen years old and my mom said to me, "Someday a man is going to tell you your eyes are beautiful. Don't fall for it."

"Thank you, Juan," I said "but don't you feel it was just a tiny bit wrong, forging a loan on an old woman's house so she'd get stuck with a million-dollar bill she couldn't possibly pay? And wouldn't it have been a tiny bit awful if she'd ended up homeless because of it?"

By now Juan knew I wouldn't buy his spiel. His blue eyes went hard as icy steel when he looked at me. "If you can't be tough, then you can't be successful. This is the way all great men make it in America, sweetheart. Your husband here knows it, and my son damned well knows it. America has winners and losers, baby, and we are the winners. If she'd lost her home, she would've been one of the losers. It's that simple."

"Ah! It's a male thing!" I laughed, sipping wine. God, he was a jerk! I was disappointed that Juan and Kidd hadn't come closer to charming me, but I suspect even the best of them have their off days. Still, if you read the definition of the sociopath in the following chapter you'll see that Juan and Kidd fit the bill perfectly: no guilt, and no conscience; in fact, in their mind, what they were doing was beautiful and good. It's what all the "winners" in America do! If you're not willing to steal and con artist in America, according to Juan and Kidd, you're a loser. You deserve to lose! The only reason Juan went to jail, in his mind, is that he was a victim of some other bad person. In his opinion, the way he operates is the way every person operates. These peoples' minds are very frightening!

Juan was indomitable, though. Despite my blatant lack of interest in his investment ideas, he still reached into his briefcase and handed Mike, not me, the prospectus. It definitely was a male thing at this point.

"Here you go, Mike. Looks like you wear the business brains in the family," (ooh, now it was a male-bonding thing) "and when you look at these figures, I'm sure you'll want to give us a call."

Mike and I poured over the figures after serving our guests a quick dessert and coffee—they had clients to meet, so they had to run—and we could not believe what we saw. For only $15,000 we would have the privilege of investing in something that may not have panned out in ten years. At the end of ten years, we would get either nothing or $1 million. To me this did not sound like a very good thing, but that's because I knew from all the research I'd done on con artists that my $15,000 would go straight into Juan and Kidd's clothing fund.

The American Psychiatric Association: "The Sociopathic or Antisocial Personality"

According to the American Psychiatric Association, a sociopathic or antisocial personality is characterized by "a lack of socialization along with behavior patterns that bring a person repeatedly into conflict with society; incapacity for significant loyalty to others or to social values; callousness; irresponsibility, impulsiveness; the inability to feel guilt or learn from experience or punishment. Frustration tolerance is low, and such people tend to blame others or give plausible rationalizations for their behavior. Characteristic behavior appears before age fifteen, although the diagnosis may not be apparent until adulthood."

Sound like anyone you know? According to Frank J. Bruno, Ph.D., author of *The Family Mental Health Encyclopedia*, it is estimated that the incidence of antisocial personality disorder among males is 3% of our total population. Among females, the incidence is lower, about 1%. According to Dr. Bruno, this personality disorder is characterized by an inadequate set of moral and ethical standards. Such individuals "have very little conscience," he writes. "They have not accepted the norms and values of their culture."

The term "sociopathic personality" refers only to adults, but adolescents prone to sociopathy commonly exhibit the following behaviors: truancy, delinquency, chronic lying, drug or alcohol abuse, theft, and vandalism. By the time they're adults, their common behavior patterns are irregular employment, ineffective parenting, no respect for the law—none at all, for any laws—inability to remain attached to one sex partner, recklessness, and failure to meet financial obligations.

In the *International Encyclopedia of Psychiatry, Psychology, Psychoanalysis and Neurology*, reference is made to J.C. Prichard, who first described the condition as "moral insanity" in 1837. It is now known, the entry continues, that there is a specific genetic component to this illness in some or all cases.

Children born to all socioeconomic levels can be afflicted with this personality disorder, wealthy families seem nearly as prone to the disorder as families living in poverty. When there's a combination of an alcoholic or sociopathic father, for example—and those two conditions are not confined to impoverished families—and evidence of ten or more antisocial symptoms in the child, there is a 50% chance he or she will become a sociopathic adult. According to Dr. Bruno, too much permissiveness and emotional isolation are common to all sociopaths' childhoods, and many wealthy kids grow up in emotional isolation and become exploitative when they're older.

In 1973, B. Wolman studied the families of sociopaths and found some common threads: lack of affection in the parent-child relationship, and not much attention. The children of these families had to take care of themselves from a very early age. They developed a "sink or swim" mentality. They became selfish and narcissistic. They learned to distrust people because there was no one to relate to, or depend upon, or identify with. They saw themselves as rejected, lonely, innocent beings. Remember those last three feelings—rejection, loneliness, innocence—because many older people see themselves that way, too. Sociopaths, having experienced those feelings themselves, tap into that emotional experience. They promise older people liberation from those feelings.

As the sociopath grows up, he or she develops selfish and exploitative attitudes toward other people. A sociopath uses people as instruments for selfish purposes and despises those who refuse to satisfy his or her narcissistic needs.

The *International Encyclopedia of Psychiatry, Psychology, Psychoanalysis and Neurology* lists the following therapies for the antisocial personality disorder: psychotherapy, behavior therapy, drug therapy, electroconvulsive therapy, lobotomy, and imprisonment. But, the entry concludes, none of these have ever proven successful! Dr. Bruno thinks psychotherapy might work, but the typical sociopath would never go. "There's nothing wrong with me!" he or she would cry. Everything is everyone else's fault, and the sociopath is perfectly normal.

> "The mind is its own place, and in itself
> Can make a heaven of hell, a hell of heaven."
> —JOHN MILTON, *Paradise Lost*

How to Win Against the Con Artist

This is another lesson in rudeness. I belong to the Peace-Love-Brats Generation, and although some of us still retain traces of the ultra-refined good manners our poor parents tried to teach us, the "brat" won out in most of us. Unfortunately for the over-fifty crowd, your extremely good manners make you vulnerable. I have listened to many older victims saying, "He was so nice," or, "He had such good manners, and you don't find that these days."

I've stressed how lovely and charming these con artists can be, and therefore, how very difficult it is to win against them. You have to risk being labelled "a crabby old woman" or man in order to protect yourself. After all, one of the joys of getting older is the freedom to get crabbier and crabbier. After years of being polite and nice, you've earned that privilege; you no longer have to be sweet to a boss you don't like, for example, because you're retired. You don't have to be nice anymore just to convince people you're wonderful, because you already know your exact self-worth, and you know that the people who love you know you're wonderful. Et cetera.

Don't be a "courtesy victim." If you were taught to be gracious at all times—and this was certainly hammered into women more than men—don't be so now. If someone calls on the phone and you don't want to listen to the spiel, tell the caller you're not interested and simply hang up. Get rude. Save your sweetness and your best manners for people who love you—your friends and your family. If you feel you don't have enough of those or if too many of them have died recently, see the chapter on "Avoiding the Isolation that Makes You Vulnerable." Have a good time with peers who don't care about your money.

If a new person comes into your life who offers all sorts of help and friendship, enjoy it until and unless they want to know about your money. If he or she drives you around, helps you with chores and sits for long, lovely chats with you, savor all of it. It is important to be sure, however, that your friend is doing all these things for you of his or her own free will. You do not owe anything for it, and if someone tried to make you feel you do, tell him to go jump in a lake! And should this new friend want to "help" you by turning you on to a great deal, investment, home repair, or living arrangement, get suspicious! Don't do or sign anything until another, disinterested party advises you.

If someone flatters you at the same time he or she wants you to sign something or invest in something, you can almost bet it's a con job. I'm not saying what he or she is telling you isn't true; you probably look great for your age, and you probably do have beautiful eyes, a beautiful house, beautiful children, and good taste. But that doesn't mean you should give away your money, just because someone recognizes the truth! Find someone who recognizes how wonderful you are *without* asking for anything in return. I am again reminded of my mother's warning when I was a teenager: "If a man says your eyes are beautiful, don't fall for it." She *meant*, "Don't go to bed with someone just because he flatters you." It seems obvious; why would I do that? But I've certainly met tons of men who flatter women just to get into bed with them. The strategy must work, or there wouldn't be so many jerks trying it. The same thing applies to con artists: they will flatter just to get to your money.

Remember Chaucer's tale of Chanticleer, the vain rooster? The fox almost got him with flattery, but Chanticleer escaped the fox by turning around and using the same kind of flattery on the vain fox. It might be worth a try; I'd love to see a potential victim smile sweetly and say to a con artist, "Oh, I'm sure a man in *your* position can't possibly be interested in my measly few dollars. No, from all you tell me about yourself, I am way beneath you, sir. Good day." Click. Slam. End of discussion.

In the same vein, some people fall for a con artist because he or she "sounded so good." A swindler's entire success depends on how good he or she sounds, and con artists are brilliantly adept at combining a smooth, professional-sounding sales pitch with extremely polite manners. Swindlers preying on older people know how important good manners are to your generation and how often you lament the lack of them in today's world. Don't fall for the good manners routine! Using sweet talk to get your purse is not polite.

Just So You Know: Pickpocket Schools

Professional pickpocket schools, located in Brazil and Mexico, teach their students to target the elderly. Las Vegas, Nevada, is a place, the students are told, where they can make massive amounts of money every day. When you are standing in line for shows or buffets, or if you are part of the huge crowd watching the pirate show at the Treasure Island Hotel or the volcano at the Mirage, beware! Florida is another pickpocket's Mecca. Men, don't keep your wallets in back pockets. Put your big bills in passport holders you can wear around your neck and under your clothes. Women, fanny packs you can wear in front, secured tightly at your waists, are very popular right now, so take advantage.

Mail Fraud

Interview with
David Westberg, Postal Inspector

WHEN I INTERVIEWED Keith DeVincentis of the FBI, he suggested that I speak with Mr. David Westberg, who is his Postal Inspector counterpart. Westberg has been in this position for seventeen years. He conducted numerours spin-off investigations after Operation Disconnect and did important victim interviews associated with the California Rolling Labs case, and has been actively involved with many other huge cases. His knowledge of the history of scams and the psychology of con artists and victims is vast, as well as fascinating. We spoke on the phone for hours.

After Operation Disconnect (see page 71), many of the telemarketers began running their schemes under cover, using mail drops and calling from phones at numerous locations, including motel rooms, various personal addresses, and cellular phones from almost anywhere. Some of these schemes promised to recover funds that had been taken from victims in earlier telemarketing scams; but they required the victims, most of whom were advanced in age or in poor health, to pay hefty up-front fees—often several thousand dollars. The fees, some of the victims were told, would go toward the taxes on the amounts to be returned to them, which were, according to the pitches, already set aside for them and ready to send out as soon as the fees were received. Many victims were hit on over and over again by similar recovery schemes.

The Rolling Labs case was a scheme wherein persons were called on the phone and offered free medical examinations, only to have their insurance companies bilked for thousands of dollars for tests that were either unnecessary or never even performed at all. (For more information on the Rolling Labs case, see page 104 in the chapter "Health Fraud.")

"What are you working on right now?" I asked Westberg.

"Telemarketing investment scams. They run the gamut. Across the country there is a community—a network—of con artists who for the last fifteen to twenty years have represented fifteen to twenty companies. Today, for example, I was in court on the Rand Bond of North America case." In that case, more than six hundred investors lost approximately $8 million. Many of the Rand Bond salespeople had previously worked at other over-the-phone precious metals investment companies that had either "busted out" or otherwise been shut down by either criminal prosecution, civil action, or both. "It's frustrating, of course," said Westberg, "because the defendants rarely get the sentences I'd like to see, and caseloads relating to telemarketing companies in Las Vegas, Southern California, and Florida are especially heavy."

"How have the investment scams changed over the years?"

"In the seventies it was swamplands in Florida, then the deserts. Then came the timeshare scams, then diamonds. I did a lot on those two. After that, along with the big Wyoming and Alaska oil leases, came the oil-well scams. Then, through the rest of the eighties, precious metals and limited partnerships became the investment scams of choice. The con artists are all the same. They're very charming. They always smile and shake my hand when I arrest them, and then they start telling me their stories. Good stories.

"It's frustrating, very frustrating for me to see persons get off lightly who have committed the most vile of offenses and brought to ruination the lives people have built for themselves."

"What about restitution?"

"Restitution is rarely made. First of all, it's a pain in the neck to administer and collect, which is a responsibility of the Department of Justice; but secondly, and perhaps more significantly, the money is usually already spent by the con artists—on fancy cars, gambling, booze, drugs, and women (but, yes, on men too, because the con game is not a male-dominated occupation). In those cases where there is money available, it is usually sequestered by the con artist, who professes poverty when facing the court."

"Why do you handle telemarketing fraud here, at the Postal Inspection Service?"

"Most schemes involved with 'wires,' which includes telephone calls, also involve the use of the mail. When the victim sends in his or her payment, it is usually by mail, and is a chargeable mail fraud count."

"Do you have any advice for consumers who get something suspicious in the mail?"

"Throw it away."

Westberg went on to relate the story of two elderly widows who had both been victims of previous telemarketing companies. One had invested with Glatin, London Metals, and a third company; the other's husband, recently deceased, had invested with Noble Metals. A former salesperson of these companies, who had also worked for several other precious metals companies, including Rand Bond, called the two women and claimed that he was an attorney representing the investors of London Metals in one case, and Noble Metals in the other; he said he had filed a lawsuit and expected to get a judgement in favor of the investors. He explained to each of the two women that he was calling them because he knew they had invested large sums and that their particular circumstances—being recently widowed, in poor health, and senior citizens—would make the courts sympathetic to them. "The two women did lose money," Westberg said, "but the last additional payments were made following a couple of tape-recorded conversations, and the money sent was my money, not the victims', and we were there with search and arrest warrants when it was to be delivered.

"Con artists are the world's best psychologists. They'll home in on your weaknesses. If you're religious, they'll throw in a million 'Praise the Lord's. If you're a family man they'll tell you they've got four kids at home. I seize all their training tapes, so I know what they're taught: if they can keep you on the phone, they'll get you to like them. They are quick on their feet, have excellent communication skills and magical wits. They'll keep you laughing if you don't know what they do for a living. Just don't let them near your money. It doesn't matter *what* they're selling! If you like them, you'll buy it.

"I had another victim, a man who was a wealthy flower grower. Over a period of fifteen years, one of these con artists nurtured enough of a relationship with this lonely man that he was able to take hundreds of thousands of dollars. The elderly flower grower still misses his long-time 'friend,' now twice convicted of mail fraud.

"Seniors are targeted by con artists because more of them suffer from short-term memory loss," Westberg pointed out. "Sometimes this is a function of age, sometimes of medication. With short-term memory loss it becomes difficult for the victim to pick up on inconsistencies in the pitch. They also do not make good government witnesses, and the con players know this. If the victim is in poor health, even if the memory is sharp it is difficult for the government to require the victim to travel across the country to testify. Con artists know this too. Just as important to the con artist is the fact that some seniors are sitting on nest eggs."

"What about solutions, something you would suggest right now that would make a difference?"

"Don't restrict the courts in sentencing. Judges see these cases every day, and should be given back the power to sentence appropriately."

How to Avoid Mail Fraud, and What to Do If You Get Hit

As David Westberg made clear, mail fraud and telemarketing go hand in hand, so everything relating to telemarketing is true of mail fraud. Nevertheless, some crimes are committed in the mail first. For example, I spoke with Lora McKay, a Financial Services Representative at First Interstate Bank, and she told me of a very common way older people are approached by con artists through the mail.

McKay told me about a woman in her eighties who kept getting postcards in the mail saying, "You've won $1,000. Sign here, write your credit card number and bank account number, and we'll deposit the money in your account." When this woman received these cards, she brought them to the manager of the First Interstate Bank where she did all her banking, and he ripped them up for her.

Many mail scams revolve around contests you may have won, and the bottom line here is, if they want you to pay one dime—for charity, for "tax fees" or for any sort of "service charge," they are probably bogus. For example, I recently received a very authentic-looking check for $7,500 made out to me. An accompanying letter said I could get this check "validated" by calling a 900-number. Upon closer examination, I was infuriated to read the extremely tiny print stating the phone call would cost about $25.00! Don't fall for it; you should never have to call a 900-number, which is very expensive, when you win a prize. In another common scam, you receive an official-looking document stating you've won a camera or some other decent prize. They want you to mail about twelve dollars to them for some fee. Don't do it.

Your U.S. Postal Inspection Service has a representative right in your local area who will be more than happy to advise you if you think you may really have won something. Take the postcard to your local post office and see what your inspector thinks. Also, ask your local U.S. post office for the free booklet the U.S. Postal Inspection Service recently completed on sweepstakes, contests, and prize promotions. It will give you handy guidelines.

Basically the rule is, if you've won a contest, you'll know it when you get the check in your hand. You should not have to do a thing or spend a dime to get that check.

Other kinds of mail fraud that especially target those over fifty-five include false billings, insurance deals that sound too wonderful to believe (they are!), land and advance-fee selling swindles; franchise schemes; work-at-home and fraudulent diploma schemes; charity schemes; promotions for fake health cures, beauty devices, fast-working diets, sex stimulants; chain letters; lotteries; and solicitations for the sale of advertising specialty items.

Remember, 92% of all American households have been hit by at least one of these schemes, so they probably sound familiar to you. While researching this book, I allowed myself to stay on the phone while four different people called me, with extremely high-pressure sales tactics, to enter the Australian lottery. I'd received a postcard in the mail prophesying my winning eleven million dollars, tax free. Two days after I got this card, they called me on the phone. All I had to do was spend $89 on my credit card and I would get 5,000,000 entry chances (or some other equally absurd number) in the Australian lottery. According to these salespeople, I had a one-in-five chance of winning eleven million dollars.

"How can you pass that up?" they asked me.

"Because nothing in life is that easy!" I shouted at them. After hemming and hawing, I said no to the first salesperson, a woman. One hour later, I was called by the second salesperson, a man. They spoke to me as if their lives depended on my spending that $89 on my credit card! At one point I imagined a gun was being held to their heads: "She'd better buy," I imagined some sleazy guy saying to them. But by the time the fourth person called me, I started to feel as though someone would appear at my front door with a gun! These people were not going to stop bothering me. At one point, the fourth guy said, "What's the matter, you don't like winning money?"

"No," I said. "I don't like getting ripped-off, which you people are obviously trying to do. I have tape recorded my conversations with all four of you, and I am giving the tapes to my Attorney General."

I was astounded by the salesman's response. "One-party-consent tapes are not legal in your state. That's why we phone there," and he hung up! (He was correct.) Thankfully, I never heard from the lottery people again. Throw those foreign lottery ads away; the chances are too good it's a complete scam! Chain letters never work, so throw them away, too. Anyone sending you a flyer about selling land or selling your timeshare should be highly suspect, so if you don't feel sure about it, ask your Postal Inspector what he or she thinks. That's his or her job.

If you feel you have been approached by a rip-off scheme via the U.S. mail, there is a toll-free Postal Crimes Hotline you can phone twenty-four hours a day: 1-800-654-8896. Or stop in at your local post office and ask to see the local Postal Inspector. If he or she is not on the premises, you can ask for the phone number where he or she can be reached. The address of the Chief Postal Inspector is: The Chief Postal Inspector, 475 L'Enfant Plaza West SW, Washington, DC, 20260-2175.

Another number to call if you feel you have been victimized by a scam or if you have questions about a mail promotion is the National Fraud Information Center, at 1-800-876-7060.

Mail fraud and telemarketing fraud bring in enough money that the FBI has linked many fraudulent companies' owners to mob associates in both New York and Chicago. In 1991 the FBI cracked down on a Las Vegas company known as Crown Marketing, a telemarketing company that was offering loans for an "advance fee" via the mail and phone. They took in $250,000 before being shut down by the FBI.

If you ever receive an ad in the mail offering "fast money, no questions asked," crumple that paper just as fast as you can. The odds are too great it's a scam. In fact, David Westburg's suggestion to throw away any mail that asked you to spend money is probably a good one.

Health Fraud

Congressional Testimony of
Senator John McCain

IN MARCH OF 1993, Senator John McCain (R-Arizona) made an impassioned speech before the Senate in favor of the Telemarketing and Consumer Fraud and Abuse Prevention Act (S.568). Because his testimony so vividly depicted the tragedy of this type of fraud, I have quoted parts of his speech before the Senate relating to health fraud in America today.

"I have focused on the issue of consumer fraud for several years now, particularly on the issues of health and consumer fraud targeted at the elderly. On March 16, 1988, I testified before the Federal Trade Commission on my concern about health care and consumer fraud affecting senior citizens—leaving behind unsatisfied and, in some cases, physically harmed seniors who relied on fraudulent products and health care schemes.

"Telemarketing and consumer fraud costs American taxpayers tens of billions of dollars per year and, in the case of health fraud, can cost lives as well. Such fraud is often committed by individuals who escape legal action by dismantling their operation and relocating to begin the operation again. In the cases of these boiler room scams both the victims and the perpetrators are difficult to locate, since the operations often consist of nothing more than phone banks, which do not readily provide detailed evidence of illegal activity.

"There are several areas of fraud to which the elderly are particularly susceptible. First, health fraud is one of our nation's leading consumer-fraud and health-care problems. Older Americans as a group experience deteriorating health and a greater number of terminal illnesses than the rest of the population. In searching for a way to prolong life and combat illness, the elderly are particularly susceptible to the claims of scam operators.

"Health care fraud can be life threatening. In some cases, the so-called cure may be deadly as well. In other cases, the product may be harmless, but a victim may be led to choose the product for treatment of an illness instead of a physician-recommended course of treatment. Again, the result could be quite serious.

"Not only is such fraud dangerous to the consumer's health, it is also costly. Current projections by the National Council Against Health Fraud indicate that this activity is costing Americans close to $25 billion a year.

"A few examples from my own state of Arizona illustrate the magnitude of the problem. [One] case involved a honey cancer cure called Tumorex. The ad read: 'Cancer patients undergo a six-day therapy of daily Tumorex injections administered by a licensed M.D. or R.N. This is augmented by amino acid capsules taken one-half hour before each meal. Any enzyme program must be discontinued twenty-four hours before the first day of treatment. In most cases, six days of treatment are sufficient; however, twelve days or more are required for some severe cases. Colon cleaning is important before treatment and imperative after treatment. $2,500 includes the six-day or twelve-day treatment and transportation (meals and lodging not included). We suggest cashier's or traveler's check; however, Visa and MasterCard are acceptable.'

"Mr. President, Tumorex is really the amino acid L-arginine, which can be purchased at local health food stores at a cost of $5.50 for 100 tablets.

"Second, consumer fraud via the television or telephone is another issue of particular concern to older Americans. Medical and health services are commonly marketed in this manner. While many of the sellers offer legitimate services or merchandise, many times consumers lose by not receiving the ordered item, receiving a copy rather than an authentic item or by suffering some financial or health loss.

"One example of this type of telemarketing scam in Arizona involved a nationwide shop-at-home program. This program involved a listing of various items for sale. The money for these items was sent to the company, which, in turn, cashed the checks and never delivered the merchandise.

"Third is the area of life-care communities. While life-care communities can be a practical solution to the problem of assuring constant care for the elderly, there have been several occasions when senior citizens have lost their investments due to fraud or mismanagement. This has involved the misrepresentation of financial risks, mortgage-lenders' interests in the life-care community, and the misuse of the entrance-fee financing.

"The structure of the life-care industry facilitates such abuses, and it is time that we take a close look at the industry's practices and ensure that life-care communities remain safe alternatives for senior citizens."

Senator McCain is right on target about the most terrible ways health care fraud affects the elderly. Arizona is one of the thirteen states whose elderly (over sixty-five) population increased by 30% from 1980 to 1990, according to the U.S. Department of Commerce. New laws, such as the one Senator McCain testified to enact, will help fight the criminals; but education is the consumer's main weapon against these kinds of fraud.

Poor health is not so prevalent among the elderly as we might assume. According to a 1992 Bureau of the Census report, three in four non-institutionalized people between ages sixty-five to seventy-four consider their health to be good or excellent, as do two out of three of those aged seventy-five and over. However, Senator McCain was correct in pointing out that terminal illness strikes the elderly more frequently than any other age group in the population, making them vulnerable to promises of miraculous cures.

Even elderly people who feel good are getting ripped off by sham health-care products touting "more zip, more energy" or "boost your sex life"—always a big seller. When I spoke with Margaret Stanish, an expert in telemarketing fraud, she said that many of her victims had at one time purchased phoney vitamins and ended up on the "sucker lists" for bigger con artists with bigger rip-offs.

Nursing-home and life-care community rip-offs have been getting a great deal of media attention; the television show "20/20" recently did a special on the financial abuse prevalent in many long-term-care establishments for the elderly. The crisis of ruthless managers and workers in the nursing-home industry has, in fact, grown so severe that outcry demands an entire revamping of regulations and structure for the industry. We will see tremendous changes in the long-term-care systems in the next few years; but in the meantime, if you are looking for a long-term-care facility, for yourself or your loved one, contact the Long Term Care Ombudsman in your district for a full report on care facilities you're reviewing. At the back of this book is the number in each state for America's State Agency on Aging. Call your state's agency and ask for the number of your local Long Term Care Ombudsman. This office keeps very current on all long-term-care facilities in its district. You can ask if there have been any complaints about any facility, and if so, which complaints. Ask your Long Term Care Ombudsman for any free brochures their office has published on choosing a long-term-care facility. Go to the facilities and talk to people who live there. You cannot do enough research on these facilities; too many ruthless individuals have robbed the residents, not only of all their money, but of their dignity as well.

Health Alternatives Without Fraud

One of the most prevalent health-care scams targeting older people is the hearing aid scam. There are so many hearing-aid scams out there that I have paraphrased the following cautionary advice from a consumer guide: Beware of advertising promising "free hearing tests," and never agree to a hearing test in your home. Never waive your right to see a physician before purchasing a hearing aid. If a physician has recommended you get a hearing aid, shop around. Prices and comfort vary widely. Finally, if you do buy a hearing aid, remember that you have the absolute right to a full refund as long as you request it within thirty days of purchase.

Although Senator McCain was correct in his denouncement of a so-called cancer cure that, in reality, cured only the victims' heavy wallets, all of us know of some "alternative health" victories, once scoffed at by the Western medical profession, that are now considered mainstream. Acupuncture, for example, is now covered by most U.S. medical insurance policies. Some very inexpensive vitamins and herbs have been used successfully for thousands of years, and really can relieve minor health problems substantially. Please note my use of the word "minor." If you have a life-threatening disease, you need a specialist. Find a specialist you feel great about, and don't stop looking until you do feel great about your doctor. I've personally known several cancer patients who have completely beaten the disease, and they could not have done it without excellent cancer specialists they trusted with their whole hearts.

So how do you know if a product is legitimate and not a scam? Do your homework; when your health and your money are at stake, read everything you can on the subject. Go to your local library and look at health magazines. Look in the *Readers Guide to Periodic Literature* in the library's reference section and look under headings relating to your ailment or body part. It will list every recent article on that topic, in a wide variety of magazines. Also check all the medical research journals put out by the American Medical Association and different schools of medicine to see what latest discoveries have been made.

Then do research in alternative medicine journals to get different views on the subject. If you're interested in alternative cures for various health problems without any hype or sales talk, one alternative medicine journal is called *Alternatives,* written by Dr. David G. Williams. It's an inexpensive journal, and he is selling nothing; he has no financial stake in any of the plants he researches. He also tells his readers how to find the purest and very cheapest form of the vitamins, herbs, etc., about which he writes. He writes about herbs and techniques from all over the world that have been shown to relieve minor health problems, and readers write in with their own kitchen remedies, which require more cleverness than money. An example of his no-frills, no-fraud, no-hype articles is "The Poor Man's Homemade Anti-Smoking Device," (volume 5, no. 9, March 1994), and he tells you how to make the device yourself. Dr. Williams also wrote a six-page article filled with data touting soybeans as a remarkable cancer preventative for colon, breast, lung, and prostate cancers. Soybeans are a lot cheaper and better for you than Tamoxifen! This is the kind of "alternative," preventative medicine that doesn't rip you off. You can call 1-210-367-4492 to inquire about the journal, which is published in Texas by Mountain Home Publishing.

If you are interested in vitamins, herbs, and other "natural" cures for sex problems, lack of pep, obesity, or quitting smoking, take a trip to your local bookstore. You will be amazed by the variety of titles on the subject of healthy, natural boosters. Anything promising a "total cure" should be suspect, but eating better, exercising, and maybe a vitamin or herb can perhaps boost your health.

What you will also notice, should you pick up an herbal guide, is the number of times certain herbs are mentioned. If your interest is piqued, or if a friend of yours swears that garlic and echinacea help her kick a cold every time, you might want to give them a try. Garlic may boost your immune system. It won't "cure" you, but it tastes good, it cannot hurt you, and it's very cheap. You can even buy it already mashed in your produce department. If you investigate further, the next thing you'll notice is the abundance of cheap supplements you can get at your local bargain drugstore. There is no need to buy expensive, fancy varieties someone is pressuring you to buy, when the most bargain-oriented drugstores in your area sell the same products for tremendously less!

If the plants themselves become interesting to you, you can take a class at your local community college on how the Native Americans in your area used local plants for healing all varieties of ailments. You may end up growing your own aloe vera on the windowsill. You can tear off a piece when you get a scrape, burn, or allergy rash.

The important thing is research and education; anyone who approaches you with a hype should be suspect, and any cure-all that costs a fortune is very likely a ruthless rip-off. Most of these expensive miracle cures—*especially the ones accepting only cash or cashier's checks, or only accepting cash via Western Union*—will do nothing for you except take your money. Don't let people prey on you. Use your library to learn everything you can about your body and what may or may not make you stronger. The information at the library is not for sale, so it can be objective.

On the subject of healers, here's a good story about a Chinese healer who definitely was more interested in his clients' health than in taking their money. He had a small pharmacy in the San Francisco Bay area, back in the late seventies. I don't think he was more than fifty years old, although I heard him tell some people he was seventy. Behind his place at the cash register were boxed packages of herbs with Chinese letters all over them. On the other side of him, glass jars filled with dried Chinese plants, also labelled with Chinese characters, lined the wall from the floor to the ceiling.

I was attending Stanford University at the time and was having stress-related health problems: insomnia and stomach cramps, to name two. This jolly Chinese healer never prescribed any esoteric herb for me; rather, he always said, "Run around the block. Best way to cure student-stress." My friends and I enjoyed watching him with other clients, because his prescription was always the same.

"I can't sleep," a customer would complain to him.

"Run around the block. Best way to sleep better," he'd tell them.

"I have no energy," another customer complained.

"Run around the block. Best way to increase energy," he'd tell them.

"I'm too fat," yet another customer would complain.

"Run around the block!" he shouted. I'm not sure how he stayed in business, but I often think of him and his one prescription. The lesson I learned (and my point): the real healers of the world really want to heal you. They don't want your money so much as they want the inner happiness they'll receive when you are well. That may sound corny, but I've met enough real healers to tell you they exist, and you deserve a good one. Don't stop looking until you find a good doctor who really cares. When you go looking for a doctor who heals, you need to believe in the "heart" of the doctor as well as in the medicine. The more you know about the disease, the healer, and the medicine, the more at ease your body can be, and the healing can begin; disease is after all, the opposite of "at ease." Educate yourself, and be good to yourself. Don't let the con artists get you when you're ill.

On this subject, if you haven't read Dr. Bernie S. Siegel's book, *Love, Medicine, and Miracles,* you should do so. Dr. Siegel is a cancer surgeon who teaches people how to use their minds and hearts along with traditional Western medicine to get well. The same goes for Norman Cousins' *Anatomy of an Illness*—a must-read, reminding us that laughter is an amazingly powerful medicine. Both these authors feel Jesus really was onto something when He said, "Heal thyself." Laughter, love, and happiness are free.

The Rolling Labs Case:
Another Form of Health Fraud

David Westburg, the Postal Inspection Service supervisor I interviewed in an earlier chapter, said evidence-gathering for the Rolling Labs case took five years. The case is especially important to those over fifty-five because it illustrates how easily phoney doctors can harm your health and screw up your life. The case also illustrates how much money health-care con artists can make, and how serious law enforcement is about cracking down on these criminals.

Michael J. Smushkevich, forty-seven, an immigrant from the former Soviet Union, and Bogich Jovovich, forty-six, a Yugoslav national, are each serving a minimum of twenty years in prison in the Rolling Labs case, which is said to have generated more than $1 billion in fraudulent medical billings as well as the payment of $50 million in fraudulent health insurance claims by private insurers and government programs.

The two criminals were each ordered to forfeit $50 million and all of the assets of the medical enterprise, and had to pay an additional $41 million—totaling almost $200 million—in restitution to government programs, health insurance companies, and employee benefit plans their criminal activities victimized. (Another defendant in the case, David Smushkevich, still awaits sentencing, but more money may yet be recovered from him.)

The National Health Care Anti-Fraud Association's chairperson, Steward E. Uhler, is the Director of Special Investigations at Pennsylvania Blue Shield. He said, "The Smushkevich brothers and their accomplices not only carried out massive fraud, they preyed in the most cynical way possible on people's concern for their health and their trust in our health-care system."

Carried out over a period of ten years and spreading from southern California to four other states, their scam worked like this: they used telemarketing and other means of soliciting persons with health insurance to take advantage of "free physical exams." I quote directly from the National Health Care Anti-Fraud Association's report on the Rolling Labs case: "The perpetrators then subjected those individuals to a wide variety of tests—many conducted by unqualified personnel—and, based on the insurance information they obtained, later fabricated symptoms and diagnoses under which they submitted thousands of false claims to the patients' insurers.

"In many cases, those fabricated symptoms later resulted in insurability problems for those patients. In others, the perpetrators gave clean bills of health to persons whose test results indicated serious health problems.

"The case was the first in the country in which a defendant involved in a health-care scheme was prosecuted under the RICO law, which requires the forfeiture of all ill-gotten gains of the racketeering enterprise."

To demonstrate how many interstate agencies can be brought together on a case of this size, here are the agencies involved in cracking this case: The U.S. Postal Inspection Service, the Department of Defense Criminal Investigative Service, the Criminal Investigation Division of the Internal Revenue Service, and the California Department of Insurance Bureau of Fraudulent Claims. Assisting were the U.S. Department of State, the FBI, the office of the Inspector General of the Department of Health and Human Services, the Medical Board of California, the Ontario Police Department and the Los Angeles County Sheriff's Department. Two Assistant United States Attorneys, Lee Michaelmas and Mark Hardiman, jointly prosecuted the case. Law enforcement was very serious about ending the Rolling Labs business, and when agencies work together in this manner, crimes can be stopped.

This kind of health-care fraud—where phoney or real physicians take advantage of patients in order to rip off insurance companies—took in about $30 billion to $50 billion in 1994 alone, according to the National Health Care Anti-Fraud Association. The amounts of money are so vast with individual perpetrators it's easy to see how the dollars mount so rapidly. One Florida physician and his wife pleaded guilty to filing more than $800,000 in false claims with private payers and Medicare. In another case, a clinical laboratory firm pled guilty to filing false claims to the tune of $110 million. But for all the crooks who get caught, many more slip away. All of you relying on Medicare know there are enough problems and doubts with Medicare/Medicaid that this kind of abuse of our medical insurance system can only hurt us, the patients and consumers.

Patterns for this kind of health-care fraud boil down as follows, according to a 1993 survey by the Health Association of America:

43% Fraudulent Diagnosis

34% Billing for Services not Rendered

21% Waiver of Patient Deductible/Co-payment

2% Other

Once again, education and awareness are the keys to prevention. When crooks steal from your medical insurance company, it ends up costing you more for insurance and medical services. Go over all your medical bills carefully and scrutinize each item. If you have any doubts whatsoever, ask questions. If a health-care product you did not order arrives at your home, call your doctor immediately. Call the sender, complain, and return the items. If explanations from the doctor's office sound fishy, don't hesitate to go over them with your insurance company or Medicare/Medicaid representative. If the physician in question is absolutely innocent of wrongdoing, he or she cannot sue you because, by law, you are protected "as long as the complaint was made in good faith." When politicians talk about "health-care reform," we know our country needs it, and here is one way citizens can begin some reform: stop health-care fraud crooks. God knows, the honest ones get paid well enough; to steal even more from taxpayers should not be tolerated!

Please, question any medical services offered "free," as in the Rolling Labs case. Victims of the Rolling Labs fraud were badly hurt, both in serious illnesses not diagnosed and in later uninsurability problems due to misdiagnoses.

Many communities hold "health fairs." Watch for them in your local paper, because at community health fairs you really can have free blood pressure taken, and a variety of free health services performed by reputable health-care workers. This is one free event where there are no strings attached. Before the health fair tent goes up, community leaders check into the reputations of those offering their services for the health fair, so you should be safe. There are also lectures on better diet and exercise, as well as free pamphlets on what you can do to improve your own health. A nice side benefit is meeting a variety of health-care providers in your community without having to pay for an office visit. If you really mingle and talk to all of them, you'll find one whose attitude you really like; it's called, "browsing for a physician."

Health Insurance Fraud

Insurance fraud can take a variety of forms, and the crime is sweeping the nation. Preying especially on older people's fear that Medicare/ Medicaid won't be enough, bogus insurance companies get victims to sign up with fly-by-night companies passing off worthless paper as insurance. These "companies" have never paid on a single claim, and never will. Sure, some of them have paid a claim or two to look legitimate, and then they take the money and run. Other companies are quasi-legal; they have tiny, tiny print that pretty much excludes them from paying anything, or they've omitted some very important details in their policies that let them, not you, off the hook.

When considering buying an insurance policy, know as much as you can about the company selling it. Always find out from your state's insurance commission if the company is licensed, or "admitted," to sell insurance in your state.

Pay attention to all the price quotes and exactly what is covered. State regulators require considerable standardization among policies so that consumers can shop around. If a company does vary from the standard policy, it must clearly explain these differences. If one company's quote is much lower, look carefully at the coverage. Use a magnifying glass to read these documents. Check the company's complaint record with your state insurance commission before you buy. Never sign anything you don't understand.

Be wary of specialized insurance covering specific diseases such as cancer. Generally speaking, the narrower the coverage, the less valuable the policy and the less likely it is that the company will pay. Check the company's complaint record.

And of course, what's true for health insurance is also true for automobile, property, and liability insurance. Beware.

Guidelines to Protect You Against Health Fraud

- Ask yourself if the person or ad offers you a quick and painless cure. If so, it's probably not legitimate.

- Avoid "special," "secret," "foreign," or "ancient" formulas available only by mail and/or only from one supplier.

- Don't buy products when testimonials or case histories are the only proof they work.

- Be suspicious of claims that miracle cures or scientific breakthroughs have been held back by the government or medical establishment.

- If you're really unsure about a product, you can call the Consumer Health Information Research Institute hotline at 1-800-821-6671.

Investment and Securities Fraud

Avoiding Rip-Offs:
Elizabeth Slawinski-Messick

Elizabeth Slawinski-Messick is an account executive who specializes in retirement planning both from her office in Beverly Hills and from her home in La Jolla, California. I met her in her office at Dean Witter in Beverly Hills and began by asking her how she came to be so involved in the fight against financial abuse of the elderly. After almost apologizing for the fact that she is young, she explained.

"When I was growing up in Colorado my parents owned a retirement center, so I saw a large number of elderly people being financially abused. I saw families trying to get their elderly relatives committed—people who had full capacity—just so they could take all their money."

She was so alarmed by the tragedies she saw occurring in Colorado, she joined the Coalition Against Financial Abuse of Seniors (CAFAS). As her master's degree was in International Business Finance, she served on that multi-disciplinary team as the securities and insurance expert. Her family's background in the assisted-living care business made her an invaluable asset to CAFAS.

"To really make a difference with this kind of abuse," Slawinski-Messick said, "you have to get the public and private sectors to work together."

When she moved to California, she contacted John Coyle, a Human Services administrator for the Los Angeles County Area Agency on Aging, and asked if there was a similar multi-disciplinary group fighting against financial abuse of the elderly in Los Angeles. It was John Coyle and Elizabeth Slawinski, then (she very recently married

109

Mr. Messick), who initiated and later helped develop the award-winning FAST—Fiduciary Abuse Specialist Team. Elizabeth serves on the Los Angeles team as the securities specialist, and is very proud of it. Her commitment to stopping financial abuse of older people is endless; her calm energy is also endless.

"Can you give me an example of an abuse situation you were personally able to stop?" I asked.

"Yes, and I felt really good about this. I had a client, a ninety-two-year-old woman. Before her conservatorship was implemented, an unscrupulous insurance salesman sold her a whole life policy—at ninety-two, can you imagine? He lied about her date of birth. Noticing that he listed an incorrect date of birth, I contacted the conservator's attorney and explained that the insurance salesman falsified the contract to make a commission. Selling a whole life policy to a ninety-two-year-old is simply a display of negligence. After the attorney notified the insurance company, the policy was rescinded and the woman received all of her money back. Later we worked to have the salesman's license revoked.

"There was an incident regarding the fraudulent use of bearer bonds. Bearer bonds are not registered to a particular person. Investors clip coupons and get their money every six months. In Los Angeles, I was able to help the District Attorney's office successfully correct a situation where a caretaker had stolen twenty bonds with coupons valuing $400,000 from an elderly woman. To the caretaker's downfall, ten of the thirty bonds were left behind. These ten were then used to trace the stolen bonds to a bank in Las Vegas. The caretaker was apprehended when she later returned to the bank to make a withdrawal.

"We went to the bank and looked at the serial numbers and at who had been given money. We got the transmittal numbers, and got an indemnity bond. The company reissued the bonds to the elderly woman and went after the crook. He had deposited the bonds, so it was easy to track him. That's how we found out it was her caretaker. He'd deposited the money in an account in Las Vegas."

"What advice would you give people to prevent that from happening to them?"

"It is very important to deposit your stocks and bonds with a large brokerage firm. One that has 'deep pockets.' That way they will be responsible. If there is foul play, you will have legal recourse. And no one can steal your stocks if they're with a firm. Your stocks won't burn if your house burns. If you want to open up a trust account, a firm can do that with your trust documents. You'll be safe."

"How do you as an account executive feel about your responsibility toward your older clients?"

"It is my moral obligation to report any suspicions of fiduciary abuse of the elderly to my branch manager. I have prevented tragedies from occurring in the past, and will try to prevent them from occurring in the future. I can require account holders to provide written direction for all transactions. A responsible broker always checks the signature very carefully. And gut feelings help. 'Know your client!' That's one of the New York Stock Exhange's most important rules, and I take it very seriously."

"Any other advice for potential older clients?"

"Yes. When I was in Colorado and my family had the Assisted Living Care Center, I saw a lot of people give away their assets so they could qualify for Medicaid. I understand the dilemma, but if you give it to your kids, you run the risk, even with the best kids, that something will come up and they will spend it. The money might be gone! Talk to Medicaid representatives about ways of qualifying. Legislation is changing all the time, and will continue to change. Don't give your assets to someone else, because you might need that money later.

"And, of course, a living trust is absolutely necessary. My dad is a retired doctor, and I saw him go to court a few times to fight for the rights of older people who were competent but whose kids were trying to get them declared incompetent. Make sure you have a living trust, one that is drawn up by an attorney—don't try to do it yourself with a form, or it might be declared invalid—so that this cannot happen to you. A living trust can protect you."

Slawinski-Messick's background makes her more passionate about the subject than most brokers, and she wanted to talk more about the nursing-home industry. I mentioned a recent television program on financial abuses within nursing homes all over the country, and she had a lot to say about it.

"I believe that many publicly-funded and privately-funded nursing homes abuse their patients financially. Patients are sometimes kept longer and in higher-skilled, more intensive-care situations than they need. I've seen many who needed in-home care but were in the wheelchair section of a nursing home, and I ask, 'What are they do-ing here?' My fiance and I went Christmas caroling at a nursing home, and there was a gentleman who seemed absolutely fine, and I couldn't help but wonder, 'What is he doing here?' Their families don't want them. Their private funds are used up, then their public funds kick in.

"Sometimes nursing homes can operate similar to cartels. I saw this with my father, who refused to participate in that game. He wasn't given as many referrals because many self-interested physicians knew he wouldn't play their game. Additionally, the Assisted Living Care Center benefited patients, rather than doctors. Sometimes physicians have reciprocating agreements with nursing homes. Homes get refer-rals from doctors, and the nursing homes send all the patients back to the doctors who referred the homes. So there's no reason for those doctors to say, 'They don't need to be here!'—which my father did, all the time. It hurt him."

"And living trusts could help this situation?"

"Yes, because the person, when competent, would dictate exactly what's to be done with them and who they want to manage things should they become incompetent. That cannot be violated. Of course, laws and government policy regarding the elderly will have to change. And they are changing, every day."

More Securities Advice:
Interviews with an Operations Manager
and an Accounts Executive at Charles Schwab

In no way do I wish to advertise for one brokerage over another, but I did want to talk with experienced brokerage representatives in the in-vestment field who worked for well-known firms. The ones I spoke with were very careful not to make a pitch for their brokerage firms over others, and we tried to keep the investment information very general. Rather than whom they work for, the important thing is the information they shared about helping you keep your money safe.

I spoke with both Dean Witter and Charles Schwab brokers. Bill Hedges, a broker with Merrill Lynch, told me, "If I get you into an in-vestment with us and you lose money, you can sue Merrill Lynch, saying that you didn't understand the investment or that I pushed you into it. That sort of thing. You might even win and I'd be fired, so I try not to push anything. I don't have to. I'm doing just fine, without pressuring anyone. You almost have to beg me to invest, and with the riskier investments we'll make you prove you're an experienced investor, aware of what you're doing." This is important information to remember, should you be approached by someone offering a great investment deal who is not backed by 'deep pockets.'"

I also spoke with Patt Epps, whose official title is Senior Registered Representative. She has a Series 7 and 8 managerial licence, and works in Operations for Charles Schwab in its Reno Office. I wanted to concentrate on the special services and protection a brokerage firm maintains for clients.

"What safeguards does your firm offer to keep clients' money and assets safe?"

"First of all, we have to have sufficient identification from the account holder when they want to pull funds out. Without consent or a subpoena or the like, we give information only to an account holder. Clients can also put passwords on their accounts if they want to."

"Can you tell me about your company's policy about power of attorney?"

"A general power of attorney has to be notarized. We don't take any money instructions from a limited power of attorney."

"What about joint tenancy?"

"A lot of our clients have adult kids on their accounts as joint tenants with right of survivorship. Only one signature—from either joint tenant—is required on those accounts."

"Do you have a way to look at suspicious events when they occur?"

"We have a Compliance Department and a Risk Desk. They look at trading. We've had frauds where people were trading shares that weren't theirs. The Compliance Department caught them, and they also caught another guy who mailed in a phony signature, trying to trade shares that were not his."

"Are there any special services you offer people over fifty–five?"

"Yes. We offer seminars on trusts and tax-exempt securities."

"When a client is elderly, when do you become alarmed?"

"If we receive lots of requests for checks to be sent to the joint account holder rather than to the elderly person."

"My girlfriend is a broker who overheard another broker in her firm brag about how he got an elderly widow to buy stock so he could get the commission. 'She doesn't know the difference anyway,' my friend overheard him say. Why would this never happen in your firm?"

"Charles Schwab doesn't make solicited equity trades. We are not commission-paid. We're paid by salary."

"Your advice to investors?"

"Never buy from solicitors over the phone. Interview financial advisors. Ask friends who they use. Get your own financial advisor, one with a good client base. Cold-call people have no client base; that's why they have to cold-call.

"I had an older woman who was a little confused. She wanted to take funds from another firm and add to her account with Charles Schwab. They were 'non-like funds,' and I told her the tax consequences would be terrible. I told her she should leave her funds with the other firm. That's why we're successful. If I help a client do what's in her best interest, she'll remember."

The next person I interviewed at Charles Schwab was Martin Briesach, Senior Investment Specialist. Pat warned me that Marty is "windy" (talks a lot), but he loves his work, and he cares very much about his clients. He, too, is paid by salary, so if he makes no trades in a day— talks people out of risky trades, for example—his salary is the same as if he has made trades all day. Marty has a lot of older clients and is very conservative in his recommendations to them. Nevertheless, when I asked him for charts telling me about money invested, he was quick to show me how small stocks can come out on top.

"Can you show me the different investments over the years, and which investments have historically given the best returns?"

"Yes, here's a chart showing you what would happen if you'd invested one dollar at year-end 1925, and what you would have now. Current inflation would, by year-end 1993, make that dollar worth $7.92. Treasury bills invested since 1925 would give you $1.40. Long-term government bonds would give you $23.71; common stocks, $727.38; and small stocks $2,279."

"That's even including some pretty serious dips with stocks in 1929 and 1987?"

"Correct."

"What book would you recommend to new investors who feel overwhelmed by the idea of stocks and bonds?"

"There are many, if you go to a bookstore and look. But I have two here that really start at the beginning with basics. One is by the editors of *Money* magazine: *Safe Investing and Other Money Matters*, published in 1992 by Oxmoor House. Another one I like is the *Wall Street Journal Guide to Understanding Money and Markets* by Wurman, Seigal, and Morris. Look, the first page on this is 'What Is a Stock?' Both of these books give bottom-line basics in plain English."

"As someone who works with hundreds of clients, how do you feel about your firm's policies regarding the safety of your clients and their assets?"

"Even though I know who you are, if you want a check, we require a picture ID. I am not allowed to recommend specific equities. I can give information on types of investments available. Also, if someone calls up and wants to get information about an account, even if it's a spouse, we do not give that information unless there's a written consent or a limited power of attorney.

"We had someone call in saying he was the person on the account; he sold a $100,000 position. The money was still in the account. Our client got his statement and saw it'd been sold. Well, we record all transactions, so we were able to go back and listen to the tape. It wasn't our client's voice, so we had to pay back that $100,00 position for that client.

"Sometimes I'll type up a client's name and it'll flash on the screen, 'Ask for a password.' If the client doesn't remember the password I don't say a thing."

"Have you heard any rotten rip-off stories?"

"Unfortunately, yes, and many of the situations could have been avoided by simply meeting with the person rather than doing business over the phone, as well as never making rushed decisions to buy or sell something. That's why it's so important, if you do use an individual advisor, to make sure he's a registered RIA. Call the Securities Division in your state."

"Would you say you've developed relationships with your clients?"

"I have many relationships with my clients. We have to be protective toward our clients. I keep my investment assistance general, and I would never divulge information about one client to another client."

"Do you have any advice for new widows whose husbands left them assets but no hands-on knowledge?"

"Yes, and a lot of my clients have been in that exact same predicament. I have to tell new widows to go meet their brokers, wherever they are. Talk to a broker in person and restate your goals, which may be different from your late spouse's. Focus on your knowledge and risk tolerance. That's very important.

"I may be prejudiced, but I've had widows come in to me after their husbands died. They'd gone to their husbands' brokers, who told them 'Buy this, sell that,' getting the commissions on both ends. So I have to say I'd look for firms where the brokers are salary-paid. They don't get commissions.

"For widows who want the most secure investments, U.S. treasuries may be appropriate. These widows have enough going on at this time in their lives. They don't need to worry about risking their assets.

"I had a situation where one of my clients wanted to take out a large amount of money, $200,000, and send it off to Canada for some investment. I asked her a few questions. 'Do you realize the risk you are taking, sending all this money to someone you don't really know? Do you know any other people or friends who are investing with this firm? If yes, have you talked to them lately? Please, let me research this investment for you.' Some broker she didn't know had called her on the phone with this hot investment idea. So I asked her, 'Did this broker you didn't know explain to you what a very risky investment this is?' The risk was incredible, even if it was legitimate. I strongly encourage investors to do basic research about a company before sending money. Many times they find out they could meet their investment goals without taking as much risk."

10 Tips on How to Avoid Investment Fraud

1. Don't be a "courtesy victim." If you are part of the generation taught to have good manners at all times, untrain yourself when it comes to the telephone. Con artists are trained to take advantage of people with good manners. Hang up on strangers who want to take your money.

2. Check out strangers touting strange deals. Say "No!" to any in-

vestment professional who presses you to make an immediate decision or gives you no opportunity to investigate them, their company, and the investment. Call the Securities Division in your state to see what this person, the company, and the investment is. If the caller is extra-friendly, beware! If you are lonely and need a friend, do not seek friendship from those who really only want your money.

3. Always stay in charge of your money. A stockbroker, financial planner, or telemarketing con artist will often be "more than happy to handle every detail," thereby "relieving you of your worry." Don't let it happen! Beware of financial planners who try to get you to put your money into something you really don't understand, and don't leave everything in anyone else's hands. Stay aware constantly of where your money is and what it's doing. If you don't understand investments, educate yourself, or involve a family member or a professional, such as your banker, before trusting someone who wants you to turn over your money.

4. Never judge integrity by how the person "sounds." Con artists are professionals, and they are trained to sound smoother and better than anyone. Their manners are perfect. They are, says David Westburg, Postal Inspection Service Supervisor, "the best psychologists in the country." Good manners have nothing to do with personal integrity, and how a person sounds has nothing to do with the soundness of an investment opportunity.

5. Watch out for salespeople who prey on your fear. Con artists know that many seniors worry that they will either outlive their savings or see all of their financial resources vanish overnight as the result of a catastrophic event such as a costly hospitalization. As a result, it is common for swindlers and abusive salespeople to pitch their schemes as a way for seniors to build up their life savings to the point where such fears are no longer necessary. Remember that fear and greed can cloud your good judgement and leave you in a much worse financial picture.

6. Exercise particular caution if you are an older woman with no experience handling money. Con artists' main targets are widows over fifty-five. Women of this generation often relied on their husbands to make financial decisions. One excellent resource available nationwide is the Women's Financial Information Program of the American Association of Retired Persons (AARP). For more information, call 1-202-

434-6030, or write to Women's Financial Information Program, AARP, Consumer Affairs, 601 E. Street NW, Washington, DC, 20049. (Also, see the chapter on financial investments and securities.)

7. Monitor your investments and ask tough questions. Insist on regular written and oral reports from those you've entrusted to manage your investments. Do not permit a false sense of friendship or trust to keep you from demanding what is your right to demand. Never listen to anyone tell you that, "Oh, we do this all the time. This is a completely routine practice." If you have suspicions, call the Secretary of State Securities Division in your state and make a complaint.

8. Look out for trouble retrieving your principal or taking your profits. If a stockbroker, financial planner, or other individual stalls when you want to pull out your principal or even just your profits, they may be trying to cheat you. If anyone is pressing you too hard to "roll over" profits into new and more alluring investments, you should get suspicious. Principal or profits should be readily available to you— it's your money!—so if you're having trouble getting your money, call someone immediately.

9. Don't let embarrassment or fear keep you from reporting investment fraud or abuse. Seniors who fail to report that they have been victimized in financial schemes often don't report because they're afraid they'll be judged incapable of handling their own affairs. They're sometimes even afraid they'll be institutionalized because of it. Con artists know all about this fear, and they use it! While it is true that most money lost to con artists is rarely recovered, there are cases in which some funds are recovered. Sometimes a civil lawsuit can recover all the funds. It is in your best interest, then, to report. You won't be judged incompetent merely because you were conned; a lot of highly competent people are swindled!

10. Beware of "reload" scams. When older people who can't return to the workforce have their money taken, panic sets in. Con artists are well aware of this panic, and that's why they are so successful at hitting victims two or three more times on the promise of helping them "recoup" what they lost the first or second time. Seniors go along with such schemes, called a "reload" scheme by con artists, because they are so desperate to get back the money they lost the first time. The con artist will call saying he or she is an attorney trying to help you get back the money you lost or has a new scam that will not

only get back what you lost before, but will double your original investment. Don't go for it! Your money is gone, so go right to law enforcement. Hang up on reloaders, and save whatever money is left. You are dealing with people who have no scruples whatsoever; they won't stop until they have every penny, so expect no mercy from them.

Safe, Easy, Profitable Investing for Anyone Over Fifty-Five

A lot of older people these days are terrified by the prospect that they will eventually outlive their supply of money. This is a legitimate fear, as we are living longer nowadays than we ever dreamed possible. So common is the fear of dying broke that many con artists use it as the basis of their "get-rich-quick" schemes. But remember: the only person who gets rich quick from these schemes is the con artist himself. The best way to avoid being tempted to "get rich quick" is to manage your finances well as you go into old age.

At this stage in your life, your goal should be financial security and the peace of mind that comes from knowing you're doing the best that can be done with your money. By planning well you will remove the fear that makes you vulnerable to being conned. You will feel confident that you have chosen the safest way to assure that your money will outlive you.

Plan Ahead

Without careful research and thought beginning in your younger or young-older years, you very well could outlive your money. You probably know people whose savings have been wiped out by health catastrophes. In fact, according to a study published in the *New England Journal of Medicine* in 1991, at age sixty-five there is a 43% chance that you'll spend some time in a nursing home at some point in your life. Most likely it will be a short stay, but according to the same study there is a 24% chance that you'll be in a nursing home for over a year. Medicare stops paying for nursing homes after 100 days, and Medicaid doesn't kick in until you're pretty broke, so you must plan ahead for possible expensive disasters. Long-term care insurance is a good idea for older persons—especially those who have many assets, as it is not particularly cheap.

All of the seniors I have spoken with figured they would die at about the same age as the parent of their gender died, and financial panic set in when, years after that age, they found themselves very much alive! Forget how old your parents were at their deaths; during the past century in the United States, life expectancy has increased by thirty years to its current level: seventy-one years for men, seventy-eight years for women. If this rate of increase continues, you can expect your life span to lengthen by two days for every week you live.

In order to figure out your financial needs after retirement, it would be convenient if you knew the exact date you will die. Since that is impossible—and believing a fortune-teller or some other soothsayer is a very bad idea—you have to approximate. The United Seniors Health Cooperative has a formula they recommend: take the average of your two parents' ages at death (if they died of natural causes) and add five years. I suggest you add ten years to the average; it's better to have money left over when you die than to come up short.

Everyone beginning a financial plan for himself or herself must begin by figuring out exactly what he or she is worth. Add up all your assets: your house (the house's value minus the mortgage gives you the equity), your car (its value minus remaining payments), stocks, annuities, real estate appraisals, and your cash minus credit card balances. While you are gathering and adding up this information, make sure you have it all together in a well-labeled file, along with your will or living trust and and your life insurance policy. Store copies as well, and tell your spouse and adult children where all these documents are. Any time any of these changes, be sure to update this permanent file.

After figuring out exactly what you're worth, estimate your income. Add up your fixed income and your variable income—that which changes from month to month. Looking ahead, how do you see this income changing? To give you an idea of what you'll be receiving after you retire, your local Social Security office has free booklets you may find helpful: "Thinking About Retiring?" (SSA publication #05-10055); "Your Social Security" (SSA publication #05-10035); "How Work Affects Your Social Security Checks" (SSA publication #05-

10069); and "Estimating Your Social Security Check" (SSA publication #05-10070). You might also want to contact the personnel office of the place in which you work and discuss with them what your benefits might be after retirement.

Next you should figure out exactly how much you spend. If you are nervous about dwindling resources and you know you should be putting away more, take a hard look at what you are spending. Where is your money going? Take a look at all your canceled checks from the last year. Do you see some "problem" spending areas? Could you be saving and investing more toward your retirement if you spent more wisely? Maybe you could save more money simply by changing some old habits. Small changes can make a big difference in all spending areas of our lives, so look closely at those canceled checks.

Food is a big expense, for example, and you might find you have to put more effort into not going to the market when you're hungry. It is amazing how money can vanish in a market when you are starving! When they're roasting chickens in the deli and baking bread in the bakery, if you're hungry you cannot be expected to withstand the temptation. Shop only when you're stuffed. Magazines and paperback books could be read at the library, for example; their cost mounts rapidly. Inexpensive cosmetics have all the same ingredients as ultra-expensive ones, so the cosmetics aisle at the supermarket should be investigated. The same goes for vitamins; inexpensive ones can be just as good, so do your research on them. Buy generic drugs whenever you can. When you need a new appliance, go to the library to research what recent *Consumer Reports* articles have to say about the best brand for your money. Don't be pressured into buying a service contract on the appliance; you probably don't need it. Don't run up credit card debt; pay off your balance each month, and spend cash more often.

After taking a look at what you have, what you earn, and what you spend, estimate how much you'll need to last until your death. Again, you can't really know precisely; but as comfort is the goal here, err on the side of overabundance. The bottom line is that no matter what your situation, you will need a lot of money to last your lifetime. Life is very expensive!

Your Greatest Asset: Your Home

What if, after looking at everything, you come to the grim realization that there is nothing to invest? That there are no savings, and there is no way there will ever be any savings if you continue as you've been doing? If this is the case, take a good hard look at your home. If you bought your home more than fifteen years ago, chances are it's worth much more than you paid for it. This may be a good time to ask yourself the following questions: How much will I have to spend to maintain this home? Can I do any of the work myself, or will I have to hire others to do all the work? Is it worth it, or will repair and maintenance costs devour my savings and take all of my income?

The time may have arrived when you must sell your home. Hopefully you can look at this not as a tragedy, but as a liberating opportunity. Many older people get crunched financially because they feel they must stay in their homes no matter what, and it is this attitude that defeats them. Your home is precious, and your home is filled with memories; but when it becomes a money pit, draining all hope of a secure financial future, is it really in your best interest to hold on to it so tenaciously?

Your home is your most valuable asset. Be creative in finding ways to make that asset work to give you financial security.

For many seniors, selling the home to buy a much cheaper condominium can be a glorious liberation. No more mowing the lawn or looking for reputable contractors to do maintenance and repairs; and you get a heap of cash to put into income-producing investments. Remember, you can take all the good memories with you when you leave your home, and you can still love the house that gave you all those good times as well as a secure old age.

If you are hesitant to sell your home for fear of tax liability on the capital gain, remember that you can exclude from your gross taxable income a tax-free capital gain of up to $125,000 from the sale of your home. The rules are: (1) You must have owned and lived in the home for at least three of the last five years; (2) You must be fifty-five or over; (3) You or your spouse can never have taken advantage of this benefit before, even if you were not married to each other at the time; if either of you has ever taken this benefit before, you cannot take it again now.

If selling your home is absolutely not an option for you, you can look into home equity conversion. I urge you, however, to do this with great caution. One of the ways this can be done is through a reverse mortgage (R.M.). As Americans age, according to Bob Blaney at B&C Mortgage, more and more older people will be using R.M.s. An R.M. arranges loan advances for a set number of years (a "fixed-term" R.M.) or for as long as you live in your home (an "open-ended" R.M.). The loan amount is usually 25%–80% of the appraised value of the home, depending on the homeowner's age. To repay the fixed-term R.M., you usually have to sell the home. With an open-ended R.M., the loan is repaid when the home is sold or when the owner dies.

There is also something called a "line-of-credit R.M.," in which the homeowner chooses when and how much money he or she needs for loan advances. This can be a godsend for sudden medical expenses, for example. It is important to remember that the value of your home is not included when Medicaid tallies up your assets to determine whether or not you qualify for benefits, so if you choose the R.M. and receive monthly payments, it will not affect your ability to qualify for Medicaid benefits. For more information on R.M.s, a valuable book is *Your New Retirement Nest Egg: A Consumer's Guide to the New Reverse Mortgages* by Scholen (National Center for Home Equity Conversion, 1995). To order it, send $19.63 to NCHEC, 7373 147th Street W., Apple Valley, MN, 55124. AARP also has a free Home Equity Conversion Information Kit, #D15601. Address a postcard to this kit's name and number at AARP Home Equity Information Center, EEO756, 601 E Street NW, Washington, DC, 20049.

If you have to make major improvements on your home but can't afford them now, you can get a "deferred payment loan." (See also the section "How to Finance Home Repairs Without Endangering Your Home.") The same can be done with your property taxes; a "property tax deferral" is a lien on your property; when you die, the taxes will be paid with the proceeds from the sale of your home. You might also consider a home equity loan, but please beware of the sharks in these waters! Go only to large registered lenders, and check with your local Better Business Bureau for complaints against them. (See also the chapter in this book on home equity fraud.)

Many older homeowners faced with mounting maintenance costs, taxes, and a growing inability to maintain their homes, opt for sale-leasebacks. In a sale-leaseback you sell your home to a family member or investor with a guaranteed lifetime lease. You are guaranteed the use of the home for life, and the buyer assumes all maintenance and property tax costs. You get the cash, and the buyer gets tax benefits and the house when you die.

If I hadn't heard and read about hundreds of older peoples' horror stories and case histories, I wouldn't be so squeamish about sale-leasebacks. Here are two of the mistakes older people have made in sale-leasebacks: (1) "Too-nice" parents charge way below fair market value when selling their homes to their adult children. Don't do it! You need that cash, remember? Consider a sale-leaseback only if you can get the current fair market value for your home. (2) The sellers do not use legal, enforceable procedures. In the worst story, one unscrupulous daughter paid one half the fair market value for her parents' home, then evicted her parents when their cash was gone!

Even nice people can become unscrupulous when they become financially desperate. Protect yourself. Have all documents drawn up by a real estate attorney or a large real estate brokerage. Make sure all terms are guaranteed in writing, and don't sign anything until you understand every word of every document. When it comes to business matters, leave nothing to love, trust, good will, or chance.

Another way to get cash from your home is to sell your home and live with relatives in your own self-contained unit. There is a program called ECHO, or Elder Cottage Housing Opportunity. ECHO homes are one- or two-bedroom portable units placed behind or beside existing homes. ECHO homes cost $10,000–$20,000, and offer a way to maintain some independence while still benefiting from having relatives next door. Your local Area Agency on Aging can tell you if ECHO is available in your community.

Principal-Guaranteed Investments

Okay, let's say you've done all this work to get to the point where you have money to invest. Where is the best place for those over fifty-five to invest? Again, you have many options. Your situation at fifty-five or older is different from what it was when you were thirty-five because you have to be more conservative. Now (or very soon) you won't be able to return to the workforce to earn more money, so your principal must be guaranteed.

Investments in which the principal is guaranteed are:

- Series EE U.S. savings bonds
- U.S. Treasury bills, notes, and bonds
- Government National Mortgage Association certificates (GNMAs, pronounced "Ginnie Mae")
- Certificates of deposit issued by federally insured institutions
- Insured municipal bonds
- Deferred annuities from top-rated insurance companies—those rated A or A+ by A.M. Best and Company, an independent evaluator of insurance companies.

These investments will give you good returns, and you are guaranteed, mostly by the U.S. government, that you will never lose your original investment. The brokers I interviewed for this book told me that nowadays (1995), with some hunting, they can get GNMAs with an annual return of 10% or better. The investor pays no commission to the broker to get that return; the money that broker gets is implicit in the GNMA. Ten or more percent on your money, with the principal guaranteed by the feds, is good money. Any large brokerage can buy GNMA certificates for you.

Another safe investment well liked by seniors is the annuity. It is safe, and it produces income. Insurance companies sponsor annuities, and retired people like the fact that they cannot outlive the income they get from the annuity. The tax-deferred annuity lets you invest in the annuity tax free, like an IRA, until you begin making withdrawals. A fixed annuity compounds your interest at a fixed percentage rate— a rate guaranteed for some specified amount of time—while a variable annuity invests your savings in your choice of mutual funds.

Another reason older people like annuities is that they're passed on immediately, like life insurance. Annuities and life insurance proceeds bypass probate and go directly to the beneficiaries when you die.

If an annuity sounds perfect for you, it is important to shop around in order to get the best rate on your money at the least cost. As with mutual funds, there are "no-load" and "load" annuities; in the latter a percentage of your money goes to paying various "expenses." Avoid "loads" in both mutual funds and annuities. There are many "no-load" choices, so why pay extra?

A good place to do research on annuities is the *Retirement Income*

Guide, published twice a year by A.M. Best Company, Amherst Road, Oldwick, NJ, 08858. It should be available at your library. If it isn't, your librarian will have no trouble getting you a copy.

After comparing different annuities—their rates, safety, withdrawal options, and expense fees—compare annuities with other investment options. According to a 1982 study by the National Education Association, even annuities guaranteeing an 11.5% return paid only 8% when expenses were deducted over a twelve-year period. A mutual fund known as an "income fund," or even a conservative "growth and income fund" might grow more and give you better income. Bonds such as GNMAs return your principal to you upon their maturity; with annuities, the principal is not "done" until after your death.

Avoiding the Tax Man

If you are in a high tax bracket, do some research on your own to make sure your accountant is taking advantage of every possible deduction. Your local IRS office—a real pain to reach by phone, but interesting to visit in person—has a wealth of literature on various available deductions. Scads of books have been written on doing your own taxes efficiently. Basically, the trick is to maximize deductions and defer income to future years. Retirement plans, IRAs, and Keogh plans are all vehicles for saving toward retirement, deferring income, and maximizing deductions. Be sure you understand them as well as other available vehicles. As you approach retirement age you will need to read something to understand the many complicated rules surrounding your IRA or Keogh. A great explanation of IRA rules can be found in *Finances After 50: Financial Planning for the Rest of Your Life,* which was put together by the United Seniors Health Cooperative (Harper Perennial, 1993). This is an amazing book, and it only costs $13.00.

As an investor in a high tax bracket, you may want to look at tax-exempt investments. For example, if you are the head of the household and making over $71,000 a year, your tax rate is 28%. A tax-free yield of 10% is equivalent to a taxable yield of 14.5%. That would be hard to get in a low-risk, principal-guaranteed investment! Tax-exempt money market funds invest in very short-term tax-exempt securities of states and municipalities. The return is a bit higher than a savings account, but the investment is not guaranteed by FDIC insurance the way a savings and loan account is.

Another tax-exempt investment is the tax-exempt bond mutual fund. These funds invest in state and municipal notes and bonds, and pay interest that is exempt from federal income tax. In choosing bond funds, be careful to invest in those that purchase only insured bonds. If you have begun withdrawing your IRA money, however, don't invest that money in tax-sheltered vehicles. The IRA is the best tax shelter of all.

Beware of con artists approaching you with esoteric "tax shelters of the century." I have watched older people throw away huge sums of money on shady tax-shelter scams while trying to save a few bucks on taxes. Sooner or later you just have to grit your teeth and pay the taxes. It's much less painful than losing principal on some wildly risky limited partnership. According to David Westburg, the U.S. Postal Inspector who supervises the Fraud Unit, limited partnership tax shelter scams were the number one mail fraud scams of the mid to late 1980s. Millions of dollars were conned from wealthy investors trying to save a few tax dollars. It's better to have less cash in hand and invest it wisely now than to wait ten years to find out your limited partnership was a scam, went bankrupt, and/or that the feds don't even allow any tax deduction on it and that you owe penalties! Be alert to tax-saving scams, and when you see the words "IRS approved" on an investment, beware. There is no such thing as an "IRS approved" investment; scam artists bandy these words about in order to get older investors to sign up with their fraudulent investments.

Other Safe Investments

Other favorite investments for seniors are taxable bond and mortgage mutual funds, tax-exempt bond funds, dividend-paying stock funds, and real estate investment trusts (REITs). Yes, there are REIT mutual funds, too. In fact, there is a mutual fund for every mood, risk tolerance, and personality on this planet! Mutual funds help you diversify, thereby decreasing your risk. The manager of the mutual fund is doing the diversifying for you; he or she does the daily sweating over when to buy and sell each stock or bond the fund owns.

There are many GNMA mutual funds, and the nice thing about them is that you don't have to keep track of each bond's return on principal versus the interest income paid out; you just get your income, without the paperwork headache of separating principal from interest. My conservative broker friends, who serve mostly older clients, feel that U.S. government-guaranteed GNMAs are the best way to go, and funds make GNMAs easier to handle.

Taking a Risk on Stocks

Let's say most of your money is in principal-protected federally guaranteed investments, and there is some extra money burning a hole in your pocket. You know that money invested in stocks—especially small stocks—has historically grown faster and bigger than other investment. You want to be a part of that growth. If that applies to you, it is time to begin investigating the stock market.

According to Peter Lynch, the legendary wizard of Wall Street, you should "...only invest what you could afford to lose at the racetrack without that loss having any effect on your daily life in the foreseeable future." (This quote is taken from an interview in *Modern Maturity*, January–February 1995.) Anything written by Peter Lynch will get you revved up on stocks; his two best-selling books, *One Up on Wall Street* and *Beating the Street*, tell you why you as a consumer can beat the so-called experts. His books are a joy to read, even if you don't imagine yourself ever being fascinated by the stock market. He's very upbeat, and when you read Peter Lynch, you feel as if America is beautiful and getting better. He tells you to do your own investment homework by finding a product you love enough to believe in. Look into the company that makes the product—one way is to study the company in the *Value Line Investment Survey*, which is available at your local library.

As an aging American—a member of the largest segment of the population—you just might prove Mr. Lynch correct and beat the Wall Street experts. You can look at the products aging Americans depend on more and more with each passing day and say, "Wow, the company that makes this essential product can only get bigger!" When you find that product, talk to others in your age group. Do they love the product as much as you do? If so, study the company that makes it. What else do they make? Any duds, or do they make other winners for your age group as well? How good is their management, and what is their debt situation? The *Value Line Investment Survey* tells all regarding management, debt, and profits.

Before buying stock in a company, watch the company's ups and downs in the newspaper's stock listings. Look at the different columns telling you the year's high for that stock, the year's low, and what the stock is doing now. If you know you have a winning stock and the stock goes down, that may be your cue to buy.

Remember that stocks can soar as well as plummet. The stock market can be a great way to make your money grow, but it may be only for philosophical types who have steady nerves. If you do buy stock, the experts all recommend buying with the idea of holding it for the long term.

If you can't decide on one stock, you can do the same kind of research before investing in a "growth" stock fund. The words "growth" and "aggressive" mean the fund is not the most conservative, so you should apply the "racetrack money only" rule when considering investing in them. Nevertheless, there are some mutual funds, such as the AARP Growth and Income Fund, that will grow and give you income without extreme risk. AARP has a toll-free number that members can call to speak to a mutual fund representative: 1-800-322-2282. Scudder Mutual Funds manages this AARP group, and they have a good track record. Dreyfuss Mutual Fund Group is another well-trusted company, and it offers a free retirement planner; call 1-800-DREYFUS. Fund groups this large don't need to hound you to invest, so take advantage of their free offers.

The research tools are there for you, and the options are there for you. You truly can build a safe, secure future for yourself.

An Investment Resource Guide for Women

A vast majority of the cases of financial exploitation of the elderly I've studied involve widows. As a general statistic, men die sooner than women. Wives are usually the ones left behind, and they do not know enough about the investments their husbands made.

If you are a married woman over fifty, you desperately need to learn about your family's investments and financial matters, because by not knowing you make yourself dangerously vulnerable. You are vulnerable to crooked bank managers, crooked business managers, and less-than-ethical stockbrokers and accountants, not to mention the con artists who make billions of dollars bilking widows. You must arm yourself with knowledge about every aspect of money and business.

Money is fun. Money is ladylike; in fact, women are very good at managing money. Many powerful widows throughout the world have expanded their late husbands' fortunes far beyond what their husbands envisioned. McDonald's, with its ever-expanding Ronald McDonaldland, comes to mind as a prime example. If you and your husband have built up a portfolio of assets, you should familiarize yourself with that portfolio. You should become familiar with the whole process of investing. Men, I'm not leaving you out; if your wife has the financial gift in the family and does all the money-work, then now is your time to learn about it. Enjoy, both of you.

Your local bookstore is filled with great titles on learning to manage your money. *Finances After Fifty*, by the United Seniors Health Co-operative (Harper Perennial, 1993), which I mentioned earlier, is a great workbook to help you start from scratch in organizing your financial future. If you were recently widowed, or if your husband is ill, an invaluable book is *On Your Own* by Alexandra Armstrong and Mary R. Donahue (Dearborn, 1993). It gives great insight into the emotional and financial-planning aspects of your new life as a widow.

Another way to acquaint yourself with the investment world is to comb through your supermarket's giant array of magazines and pick the investment-related magazines with the story headlines you find most appealing. *Money* and *Smart Money* almost always have irresistible articles, written in clear, plain English. They are written by normal, real people, and are fun to read. The articles are not esoteric; they are about day-to-day economic survival and the challenge of solving our economic problems and winning—getting ahead, even, and soaring.

If the magazines and books ignite a passion in you, The National Association of Investors Corporation puts out a thorough, easy-to-read manual entitled *The Investor's Manual: A Guide to Sound Investing*. It's a club, and they want you to join. Their manual has some pretty technical stuff in it, but if you've decided to get hooked, the club meetings are fairly small and are held all over the country. Most of the people—men and women—attending are over fifty, so it's a good place to meet people with similar money concerns. Different companies and the pros and cons of investing in them are discussed, as are general market trends.

Before your husband dies, you should become completely familiar with every single aspect of his business and investments. You and he should talk; there are many decisions to make now, before it's too late. If your husband has been managing the entire portfolio, he should teach you what he's done and why. He should introduce you to his broker, and he should show you where he keeps everything. If his filing system is "creative," he'll have to explain it to you. Likewise, if you are in charge of such things, you should do the same for him. You should discuss and decide, for example, what each of you wants if you become incapacitated. A living trust is the perfect vehicle for having your wishes carried out exactly according to what you desire now, as a fully capable person. (See the chapter on living trusts.) Study and learn everything, now, before tragedy and loss make it all overwhelming. Your comfortable old age depends on it.

If your husband has already passed away, you have a long, tough journey through grief before completing your financial education, but you must remain alert. Be aware that the obituary column of your newspaper is being read by people who make their livings abusing widows and widowers in mourning. Be aware, too, that probate court records are public, and con artists go through them to find intimate details about prospective victims. As soon as possible, join a local widows' support group, or draw close to acquaintances who have been through the experience. Only people who have been through the whole process of loss know what you're going through, and they can help you each step of the way.

One excellent resource to begin your journey to financial intelligence is the Women's Financial Information Program, AARP Consumer Affairs, 601 E. St. NW, Washington, DC, 20049, phone 1-202-434-6030. Or, go to your local senior center on a day when a retired investment counselor is giving free advice. Almost all senior centers have such a day, as well as a day on which local lawyers donate free legal services. Reach out; there are many resources to help you get through this difficult time, and they are everywhere. (See also the chapter on avoiding isolation.) If you have always been a shy introvert, now might be the time your survival depends on some personality changes.

Learn, and learn some more. Don't be like the woman in Texas an Adult Protective Services worker told me about: her husband had died, leaving her with a multi-million-dollar business. She announced to the accountant, "I have no interest in it, and I don't want to know anything about it. Just send me the checks" Well, one of the employees of her late husband's business eventually noticed that the figures he handed to the accountant were not the same as the ones entered in the books. This very loyal employee called Adult Protective Services and, yes, the accountant had cheated the widow out of a million dollars. The widow was heartbroken when she learned her old family friend had fleeced her, but she urged Texas authorities not to press charges. Not only was she too embarrassed, but the accountant and his family had been very close to her.

"They're like family," she told authorities, "I just can't send him to jail." So she bit a one-million-dollar bullet, as they'd say in Texas.

The moral: never tell your accountant that you don't care, and check those books yourself! Or, if you're not familiar enough with the language of accounting, have another well-established accounting firm run surprise checks on your accountant. Accounting firms do these surprise audits all the time. It has nothing to do with lack of trust; it is merely good business.

If you and your husband own a lot of stocks, keep track of them once a week. The Sunday financial section of the newspaper tells the year's high and low prices on each stock, as well as what it did during the week. Such research can be very entertaining. Chat with your broker now and then and show off how knowledgeable you are about the stock market. Read the chapter on securities fraud so that you know how to avoid it. If you and your husband own any stocks at all, the con artists know about it.

I'm reminded of Bill Flanagan, who is the Director of Litigation for Bet Tzedek Legal Services in Los Angeles. Flanagan represents many elderly victims of home equity swindlers, so he is sensitive to the vulnerability of older people. He visits his elderly, widowed mother regularly, and he always cautions her not to sign anything without letting him read it. On one visit, she told him some guy had called and said to her, "I understand you own some stock." As Flanagan had often instructed his mom to do, she hung up on the caller immediately—well, actually, she said, "My son is a lawyer," and then slammed the phone down.

Flanagan was amazed by this. "She owns exactly eighty shares of Bell," he told me. "But they found out about it on their computers, and they were after her for something."

Prepare yourself now.

Keeping Your Money Safe: Advice from Two Bank Employees

I first spoke with Lora McKay, who used to work as a bank teller and is now a Financial Services Representative with First Interstate Bank. (I chose First Interstate because they have branches in so many states.) Lora also is in charge of new accounts, so she knows many of the different department operations in her bank.

"Would you say that as a teller you have established close relationships with some of your older, longtime clients?"

"Oh, yes. You can't help but establish very close relationships with them, especially as a teller. We look out for them."

"How?"

"If these patrons don't usually make ten-thousand-dollar withdrawals and suddenly do, we ask. It's our policy—not to be nosy, but to care. It's their money, but they come to us knowing we care. We have this one older woman who brings her mail into our manager, and he throws away all the rip-off stuff where they want you to write down your bank account number. They say it's so they can 'wire prize money right into your bank account!' He just rips it up and throws it away, and she says thanks. She depends on him."

"Is there a computer code you can put on an account that will alert a teller to potential problems?"

"Yes, we have warning codes we can put on accounts. Especially if there is unusual activity going on. We'll watch it and notify first our manager and then law enforcement or social service authorities if we're really alarmed."

I also spoke with Carol Christian, who is a Customer Service Manager with First Interstate Bank. She has worked with First Interstate Bank in different areas of the country for a total of twenty years. I began by asking her about the bank's policies regarding vulnerable older patrons.

"No, we don't have specific policies regarding older patrons," Carol said. "But we try to alert our employees to possible scams so that they can alert their patrons. Older patrons do tend to be the targets for these kinds of things, and if we know a client, we know his or her withdrawal habits. We know when the client is doing something unusual, and we ask. If the reason he or she is withdrawing is to give money to a con artist, sometimes we can stop it. We know the scams."

"Can you give an example of the kinds of scams going around?"

"For example, someone will come to your home saying they are bank examiners for First Interstate Bank, or whatever bank you use. He'll tell you he suspects one of First Interstate's employees is ripping off the bank, and he wants you to help catch the thief, so if you'll just withdraw, say ten thousand dollars from this teller and bring it to the 'examiner', he'll know by what the teller does on the computer. That sort of thing. You withdraw your money, the 'examiner' is gone, and when you come to the bank, there's nothing at all we can do. Your money is gone. That happened all the time in Las Vegas.

"There are variations on that theme, where a police officer or maybe even an FBI agent comes to your door. Anyone who asks you to withdraw money from your account is no one you want to give your money to! But it's very common. If someone does come to you and ask you to do that, notify your local police department immediately. No FBI agent or bank examiner or policeman is going to ask you to withdraw your money to give them, not for any reason."

"Anything else?"

"Around Christmastime there seem to be more than the usual number of scams directed at taking older people's money. We can't keep our customers from withdrawing all their money, but we can often stop tragedies from happening."

"Have you ever acted aggressively to rescue a patron?"

"There was an old man whose in-house health-care worker was getting him to sign checks. I felt something was very wrong, and I spoke with our bank's attorney, who said it was okay to get involved. The old man was signing blank checks for the health-care worker, and I told him to stop doing that. He was obviously being abused by the health-care worker, so I notified Adult Protective Services. The old man didn't understand, and he continued signing those blank checks, so I took his checks away and closed the account. Finally the health-care worker got the message and quit. But it can be a battle."

"How else do you see older patrons being ripped off?"

"We often have a woman come in saying she's an older patron's wife, and she wants to get on his account. Well, to put her name on the account, I need a doctor's letter stating that the man is competent, and then I need the competent older man to put it in writing that he wants her on the account. And we will really study that old man's signature, believe me! I'm a little skeptical of May-December romances, myself."

Because tellers especially get to know their clients and their spending and withdrawal habits, they are in an excellent position to identify financial exploitation. At a multi-disciplinary team meeting in San Francisco attended by social service workers and various professionals in the community who work with the elderly, I was told of several such cases. Bank tellers became alarmed when elderly clients made large and frequent withdrawals. In these cases, tellers notified the local Adult Protective Services offices, and investigations were begun. The cases did prove to be ones in which elderly people were indeed being exploited, so it was very important that the tellers had reported them early, at the first signs of frequent withdrawals.

Financial institutions have an obligation to their clients not to breach confidentiality, but they also have an obligation—in many states, a legal obligation—to report suspected abuse. In states that have mandatory reporting laws, the penalties for banks that do not report are hefty. And, as the two bank employees above shared with me, they themselves feel a moral obligation to remain alert to signs of abuse.

Unfortunately, I also heard from a Texas Adult Protective Services worker about a small-town bank manager in Texas who was siphoning little bits of elderly clients' money, and another California bank teller who became solicitous enough with her elderly client that she was able to exploit the client financially.

Fraud by Friends and Family

Befrienders: New Best Friends

Florence's Story

I MET FLORENCE (not her real name) at our local recreation center; we both swam laps at the same time of day several days a week. Florence is sixty-five and, until recently, was a model. If someone told me that swimming every day would give me a body like Florence's when I grow up, I would swim laps forever. We sometimes go to lunch together, and always enjoy good conversation.

Florence is very beautiful, and wears her silver hair straight back in an elegant bun at the back of her neck. Her clothes are stunning, and she always wears an exotic brooch at the top of her silk shirts. I would feel frumpy being out with her, but she doesn't talk the way she looks. She's a funny lady, and she uses her New York accent when she tells funny stories. She made me laugh, for example, when she told me she has remained very close with her three sons' first wives. (All three sons are now remarried.)

"Just because my sons couldn't get along with them doesn't mean I have to stop seeing them!"

But when I asked her to tell me the following story for my book, she became sad. She was married to an extremely wealthy man in New York until he passed away when she was fifty-nine. Their marriage had been "lukewarm," she said, but he had handled all the financial affairs, "and our marriage was efficient." They raised three sons, she did her modeling, and he had his business.

"When he died, it hit me that I'd been in a loveless marriage for thirty years. In a way, I was free; but what do you do with that—freedom? What is it? So I worked, I puttered around. Financial matters went on as before, because our financial managers had handled everything for years, anyway. I went out some with a few stupid gropers. I was in a fog, really.

"Then along came John [not his real name]. He worked in the same law firm as my oldest boy—a lawyer, for God's sake, how can you beat that? He was forty, and I had just endured my sixtieth birthday. I felt old, like an old, dried-up widow, and he was gorgeous. He came on to me like a ton of bricks and, my God, I fell. He lit a fire in me that I never even knew existed. I'd been a perfect wife—adultery-free, although my husband never pretended to be perfect—and you know what I learned? I learned that the reason men want their wives to be faithful is so the wives don't find out what lousy lovers they are!

"Now, John, he was from a younger generation, and women in his generation have been around, so the men have to be good, you know, in bed. He wasn't good, he was awesome, as my grandkids say!

"Anyway, John and I travelled all over Europe, the Caribbean, everywhere—all on my expense account. What did I care? I was in love for the first time in my life. I felt I deserved it. But we came back from one of our lovely trips together, and there were my boys, glaring at me with big, grim faces.

"'Mother, he's taking you for everything you've got!' they yelled at me.

"'Who cares? I'm happy!' I yelled back. I knew they were right. Come on. I don't care how great I look, and how great things were between John and me. He was forty, I was sixty, and I was paying the bills. In the back of my mind I knew that if I were broke, John would find someone else. And the way we were spending my money, I would be broke pretty soon!

"The inevitable moment came, and John suggested we tie the knot, and of course, add his name to all the bank accounts and investments."

"What? How did he justify such an incredible demand?" I asked her.

"Honey, he figured he had me so hooked, I'd have sliced up my nose if he asked me to. And I might have, if the boys hadn't confronted me. So, anyway, I told John no, I had no intention of ever marrying again. I also told him we would have to start living more frugally, and that he would have to start footing some bills. That was that.

I never saw him again. I wasn't terribly surprised. I learned a great deal from it. Lost a lot of money, too—about two hundred thousand dollars. You look shocked. Don't you know men like John who need to look nice and drive nice cars? Oh, yes, he got the best, but unlike a lot of people who get taken, I got to enjoy it. He looked damned good in those clothes and in that car, which he drove out of my life.

"It hurts, but we move on. I'm wiser, and I've got a boyfriend now who's my age, and pays his own way."

Bill's Story

Bill Jones (not his real name) owned a thriving lumber company in a small but beautiful area filled with expensive real estate. When his ailing health forced him to sell his company, he was amazed by his sudden fortune. His lovely wife threw a huge retirement party for him, and he smiled into my eyes sadly as he told me about it.

"Julie [not her real name] and I were like goofy little lovebirds at that party, starin' into each other's eyes and all. We were goin' on a cruise around the Greek islands the following week, and it seemed like the whole world was rootin' for us."

Bill is a handsome man with thick, white, wavy hair and big white eyebrows. His eyes are sad and dark. He was embarrassed and ashamed of what happened to him, and I promised him over and over as I took his hand that I would never mention his real name or where he lives. He assured me, "I'm only doin' this because there's a lot of widowers out there this could happen to."

"This was not your fault, Bill. It could happen to anyone." I tried to change the subject. "Did you and Julie have a good time on your cruise?"

He laughed, and his sad face lit up with joy and love. "God! You think it's good to be young and in love? It's nothin' compared to being old and in love!" (He was blushing, and so I gave him some privacy. I think I was blushing, too.) He laughed. "Best time we ever had, dancin' on the deck—you know. A beautiful time. Then about three, maybe six months later, we found out she had cancer. She went pretty fast."

He shut his eyes tightly, squeezing out the pain and a few tears. Horrible sounds were coming from his throat. He tried to talk, and I suggested he wait until it came more easily. He forced the words from his choking throat anyway.

"I was so lost. Julie was everything to me. My daughters, my son—they came by, but I've never been real close to my kids. They were always Julie's department. They're great kids. She did a good job, but back then the father was supposed to go to work all the time. I barely gave those kids the time of day—that's the way things were back then. I asked one of my daughters to hire me a cook-housekeeper, and I wound up with Leah. I'd never boiled an egg in my life, so she was a godsend! She did everything and, man, could she cook! She wasn't gorgeous, you know, but she wasn't bad. And after a while hell, she started lookin' pretty damned good to me, especially after my eyesight started goin' bad with the diabetes."

He laughed again, in spite of his pain. He is beautiful when he smiles, his big sad eyes sparkling with humor. I told him he was brave to share all this. It was easy to see he didn't open up often.

"So, anyway, we, you know, got friendlier, and she started payin' my bills when my eyes got bad. I never doubted her for a minute—I mean, this dame was good!—until she'd taken me for about three hundred thousand grand. I feel like such a goddamned dupe! How could I have been so stupid for so long?"

He raised a palm to hit himself in the forehead, but missed, and both of us were reminded of his vulnerability. I reminded him again, "Bill, it wasn't your fault. You were lonely, and you needed help. *She* was the professional criminal, not you, and you have to forgive yourself."

"Yeah, well, I don't think I can do that," he said sadly, shaking his head. "If it hadn't been for my oldest daughter pokin' her nose in it, fightin' me all the time about Leah, God, I'd be a bag man by now." He laughed again, and I felt happy he could laugh. He's going to be okay.

How Con Artists Exploit May–December Romances

One of the worst things about getting older is the funerals you must attend—more and more of them with each passing year. Life can get damned lonely when you lose people you've loved and lived with a long time, and sometimes that loneliness can get downright desperate. Sometimes it seems as though every funeral is a reminder of your own mortality.

Making a new friend who is young is one way to escape in your mind from the onslaught of age, and a much-younger new lover or spouse is one you're less likely to lose to death. Thus many people in the December of their lives search for relationships with people whose life calendar is on May.

It sounds like a reasonable plan, but it can go badly. Too often the younger spouse takes all the money and leaves the older spouse to end life broke and alone.

I recently watched a television program, "On the Money," about financial abuse of the elderly. The announcer proclaimed that financial abuse of the elderly was "the fastest growing crime in the United States. In 1993 alone," he reported, "there were over one million complaints of financial abuse [of the elderly]." It was a very painful segment for me to watch. In it, a young woman who was the front for her family ring of criminal gypsies, went up to an elderly man and asked him for directions. She gained his trust, and told the old man her brother would invest his money for him.

"Sally," the gypsy, married the old man, who survived a massive heart attack two days later. Sally went to the old man's bank to take $50,000 out of his account, supposedly to pay the old man's medical bills. The bank would not authorize the withdrawal, so Sally talked the old man into adding her name to his account. She took every penny of his money, and the bewildered, elderly man was left in a state-run nursing home.

During the same program, another story was told. "Charlie" was an old man who had been beaten and kidnapped by a woman whom he married five days later! Apparently the same family of gypsies orchestrated this abduction, and they told Charlie if he didn't marry the young woman, he'd be put in a nursing home and the government would take all his money. At the time the segment was taped, his gypsy wife's name was on his property title and on his checks. The courts were trying to protect Charlie, who appeared very confused.

Yet another recently televised segment, this one on the program "20/20," warned viewers that another ring of gypsies had been identified. This group committed their crimes in cities from New York to

San Francisco; young women married elderly men, poisoned them, and took all their money. From all these reports, it seems we can surmise the following: if elderly widows are the primary target for telemarketing con artists, elderly widowers are the main targets for May-December romance rip-offs.

Television has shown many great programs on these rip-offs. Another that comes to mind appeared on "Unsolved Mysteries." A retired judge lived with his trusted housekeeper, Sofia, until Sofia herself was ready to retire. Sofia looked for a long time for someone to replace her as the judge's housekeeper. A woman named Andolina was hired, and she seemed perfect. She and the judge got along fine, except that Andolina was using the judge's ATM card to withdraw $300 every other day, until her withdrawals totaled $580,000! Because the judges eyes were so bad, he didn't notice that Andolina was also removing all the expensive antiques from his home and replacing them with junk.

When Sofia returned to the judge's house to see how he was doing, she was appalled by what she found and phoned the judge's attorney. Andolina escaped with $500,000 in cash and a great deal of property, but at least Sofia was able to thwart Andolina's final plan: she had been working toward getting title to the judge's beautiful home. She escaped with the cash, but the judge still has his home.

The family of gypsies uses fear, coercion, and threats, but in-home health care and housekeeping con artists do the opposite. They gain complete trust of their victims. They often isolate the victims from the rest of their families, and tell lies about the victims' families, such as, "They want to put you in a rest home so they can steal all your money." The romancing con artist, of course, uses the cruelest trick of all: love and touch. Whatever the method, however, the result is always the same: the victim's money is taken.

Wendy Lustbader, M.S.W., is a mental health counselor at Pike Market Medical Clinic in Seattle and affiliate assistant professor at the University of Washington School of Social Work. She wrote *Counting on Kindness: The Dilemmas of Dependency* (The Free Press, 1991) and co-wrote *Taking Care of Aging Family Members* with Nancy R. Hooyman (The Free Press, 1993). Ms. Lustbader lectures all over the United States on subjects related to aging and chronic illness, and I have been lucky enough to attend some of those lectures.

In one lecture, entitled "Intimacy and Exploitation," Lustbader talked about old people's craving to be held. As we all know, touching is essential to babies' development. If a baby isn't held, it fails to thrive. But it is not only babies who need to be touched: touch is a human need that never ceases. We all need physical touch. Lustbader told a story about one of her clients who spent an inordinate amount of her Social Security check on visits to the beauty parlor. Lustbader tried to tell the woman this spending was too extravagant, but when she went to the old-fashioned, local beauty parlor, she realized why the woman had to go to that salon. The luxurious shampooing and scalp massage, the shoulder and neck massage, and the social contact and gossip were things the older woman needed in order to thrive.

Lustbader says all of us have three hungers: the hunger for touch, the hunger for intimacy, and the hunger to be needed. "Con artists," she says, "are masters at harnessing these three hungers." Spouses who have lost their mates sometimes go years without being touched or hugged; Lustbader told us of one widow who had gone twenty-seven years without a hug.

Con artists know this need, and in the videos I've watched, con artists very gently touch an elderly person's knees or take her hand while they speak to her. After a while, hugs become frequent. I've heard many stories about elderly men's housekeeper-cooks who—as happened in "Bill's Story"—have sex with the bereaved elderly widower as a way of gaining his trust and furthering his dependence on them. In one case, an Alaska APS worker told the story of a May-December romance in which a known female exploiter was living with a wealthy older man. When the APS worker went to warn the old man that this woman was known for ripping off old men, he put a gun to the APS worker's head!

In every single one of the case histories I heard about telemarketing or securities fraud, the victims' hunger for intimacy and hunger to be needed were fed. On all the cassette tapes I've heard, the con artists told the victims "secrets" about himself or herself and asked advice. In the worst rip-offs—ones that take place over a period of many years—the con artists call the victim almost daily. The con artists ask the victim (usually women, in these cases) to help with advice on their girlfriend troubles or ask her to help with other secret problems at home.

I spoke with Paul Blunt, an attorney who works in Arizona. Blunt's special area of expertise is in financial exploitation of the elderly, so he's worked on a number of cases involving May-December romance rip-offs. He says it is difficult to know at first what's really going on, because an older person with full capacity does have the right to lavish money on a younger lover.

"The heirs really hate it, though, when the younger lover is taking all their mother's or father's money and their mom or dad doesn't see it or isn't doing anything about it."

That brings up the question: when is it right to step in? Wendy Lustbader gave an example of the dilemma, citing the story of an eighty-seven-year-old woman in love with a forty-seven-year-old man. She was trying to get her will changed so she could give him, not her children, all of her money. The woman had full capacity, and said simply, "But I love him!"

The problem occurs when the young lover is not there for love alone and takes all of the elder's money before he or she dies. The elder then ends up alone, heartbroken, and broke. What a terrible, fine line the people concerned must tread! How do you tell an old man or woman who is happily in love with this young "light of their life" that the lover doesn't love him or her, but just wants money? Who is the older person going to want to believe? And, as I said earlier, con artists are very, very believable, and their fiction is infinitely sweeter than the truth.

Certainly, younger people who are kind and good do fall in love with older people. They enjoy happy, loving, long-term unions, and the younger person cares lovingly for the older mate until death does them part. If you might be one of the lucky older people who's found a younger sweetheart, you should establish a living trust immediately, for many reasons. First, if your new love is a cheat, he or she won't be able to rob you. Your trust officer will manage the money in the trust, and the "sweet cheat" won't be able to get at it. The romance may soon be finished, but at least you'll know the truth, and you won't die broke. Second, if your new love is sincere, he or she is less likely to contest your wishes as to how he or she will benefit after your death or if you become incapacitated.

Mixing your financial affairs with your romantic affair is a bad idea. If you have established a new romantic relationship with someone, enjoy the romance with him or her, but get a financial advisor to take care of the financial business. Talk to your peers or your bank's manager to get recommendations for a well-established financial advisor who is registered. Don't ask your new sweetheart whom he or she recommends! Also, if a new friend or acquaintance wants to know a great deal about your finances—or asks any money questions at all— make a new friend! This applies not only to romance interests but to any new acquaintance.

Attention, men who are proud of the fact that they "can't boil an egg." Learn to cook and clean for yourself now, before your wife dies. That kind of helplessness makes you vulnerable, in exactly the same way a widow's lack of financial knowledge makes her vulnerable. Does it sound sexist and old fashioned to say that women don't know money and men can't cook? It is often the reality, and these weaknesses show up in enough case histories that I have to mention it. In another era it was understood that women took care of the home and children, and men took care of worldly matters such as investments.

My father used to joke, "If your mother died, I'd have to find another woman immediately. Someone to cook and rub my legs the way she does."

Many cook-housekeeper con artists and the in-home health care con artists take advantage of men who can't cook. It is every bit as important, then, for husbands to learn how to cook now, before and in case they become widowers—as it is for wives to learn financial matters before and in case they become widows. Just as there are financial classes for beginners at your local junior college, there are also cooking classes for beginners available to you locally. Take advantage of them.

A "befriender" scenario goes the same route as the May-December rip-off, except that sex is not involved. A befriender uses the same methods to gain complete trust from the victim. A befriender may be an in-home health-care giver, housekeeper-cook, or even a neighbor. A befriender can also be a handyman, a preacher, or a crooked investment counselor. A befriender first "gets in" by going out of his or her way to do special favors for a lonely, older person.

In her book *Counting on Kindness,* Wendy Lustbader cites the tendency of many older people to feel uncomfortably beholden to people who do things for them. As she puts it, "The one who gives help is more powerful than the one who receives it." Many older people hate this inferior position, and they insist on payment when befrienders continually offer them services. It is their way of maintaining dignity.

As we get older, however, we have to let go a little and allow kind people to help us do things we can't do so well anymore. If kind people want to help you do little things here and there, let them. It is their choice, and you owe them nothing. If you are a pleasant person to be near, then let them enjoy your company as their reward.

I'm reminded of my own father during his final days. In his earlier years, he'd been fiercely independent, a "macho" guy, but at the end he needed help doing everything. At first it was very hard for him, but when he finally let go, he enjoyed it.

"Hell, if I'd known the service was going to be this good, I would have gotten old a lot sooner," he once quipped as he watched all of us scurry around to wait on him.

A kind neighbor or acquaintance may do many favors for you and be quite solicitous, but a befriender con artist will do the same favors while asking questions about your money. He or she will make too many offers to go to the bank for you, or will have too many great ideas about investments. He or she will start to drop hints, making you feel you are giving nothing in return for all the service he or she is giving you. He or she might say bad things about members of your family or use other methods to isolate you from them. A new acquaintance who truly wants to be your friend would welcome the opportunity to meet your family. A befriender wants nothing to do with your family and will try to turn you against them. If there is a rift within your family, a kind friend will gently try to help you mend it; the befriender will spend tremendous energy exploiting and widening the rift.

When professionals and law enforcement agencies investigate such situations, the first thing they do is determine the capacity of the victim. If the victim is incapacitated, conservatorship or temporary conservatorship is established. For victims who are fully capable, the procedure is different. When a capable victim has come to love and depend on an exploiter so much that he or she doesn't care about the exploitation, professionals and loved ones must act together. With both May-December romancers and befrienders, the solution recommended by professionals is to replace that exploitive relationship with another, non-exploitive friend. The exploiter will then lose his or her hold on the victim. Furthermore, if an Adult Protective Services worker or family member is showing up all the time at the victim's house, the exploiter will be squeezed out; they work only in isolated settings. If you don't replace the befriender or romancer with another relationship, Lustbader warns, the victim will crave another.

If you think you or someone you love may be the victim of a romancer-con artist or a befriender-con artist, look in the county section of your phone book under "Social Services," for your Area Agency on Aging. In an appendix at the back of this book, I've listed Agencies on Aging for each state; these can connect you with the office closest to you. You will most likely end up speaking with your local Adult Protective Services office. Tell them you suspect you or your loved one is being taken advantage of by a befriender. They are well experienced in this area, and they've dealt with hundreds of similar cases. There is no shame, and they know exactly how to help.

Religious Con Artists

It is hard to believe that anyone could use something as intensely personal as religious faith in order to steal. Nevertheless, from fraudulent Christian preachers to weird cult leaders, religious con artists target older people to get their money. The case histories I've heard are bizarre and difficult to believe, but they all begin the same way: a bereaved or lonely older person seeks spiritual solace. The preacher evangelist very gently consoles the lonely person. Spiritual talk centered around a loving God soothes and comforts the bereaved. The con artist almost hypnotizes the victim with this comfort, and demands the victim isolate him- or herself from friends and family. Inevitably, all property is turned over to the con artist, as well as the victims' bank accounts.

In the most horrid of the cases histories I have studied, a kindly con artist impersonating a Christian preacher consoled a widow. He visited her daily, praising Jesus and saying beautifully nourishing things to the grieving woman. Soon, however, she became quite cold toward her old friends and toward her family. The title to her home was transferred to the preacher, and then mysteriously, the woman vanished. She'd been abducted, but no one found her for several years. This "preacher" had put her in a state-run rest home, and only when an old friend ended up in the same home was she discovered.

All of us need extra spiritual guidance during difficult times in our lives, and God knows you should be able to trust your local preacher to give you that comfort. However, you should be aware of certain signs telling you that this is not a true servant of God. As with other types of befrienders, there are ways to ascertain whether the spiritual counselor you have turned to wants to help you or take your money.

The first is obvious: the "preacher" mentions money. Often, however, if you are at a low point in your life, you may not really hear the little "money words." But you must stay alert enough to be aware; a person who really wants to help you get through a lonely or mourning period in your life should absolutely not be asking you for money. If a "spiritual advisor" starts asking you anything about financial matters, get away from him or her, no matter how many times he or she praises Jesus in each sentence. Jesus would not appreciate such a person using His name to get your money. Just as you should not mix money matters with matters of the heart, you should not mix money matters with matters of the soul.

In the June 1994 issue of AARP's magazine *Modern Maturity*, Catherine Collins and Douglas Frantz wrote an alarming article entitled "Let Us Prey." It is all about religious cults who prey on older Americans, and I urge everyone to look up a copy in the local library and read it. Most of us think of wide-eyed, impressionable young people as the ones who get hooked into cults, but cults know where the money is. They apparently know very well how to get to older people. It is hard to imagine a couple in their late fifties walking up to Hare Krishna dancers on the street and asking, "How can we join?" but increasingly often, sophisticated, money-hungry cults contact potential victims "...through hospitals, nursing homes, senior centers, and even [at] the homes of the sick, lonely, and other extremely vulnerable individuals," according to the authors of this article. Other places cult recruiters have gone to get victims are meditation and health-rehabilitation classes.

All of the victims described by Collins and Frantz had one thing in common: they were at a point in their lives where they needed something inside—something spiritual. They needed answers to the new problems their ages and their health presented. According to Daniel Kratz, the Director of Chaplains for Manor HealthCare Corp., a company that operates 160 nursing homes, older people in the nursing homes "...are trying to make sense of it all, to arrive at life's meaning, to see what they have accomplished." Hence, nursing homes were being combed by cult workers in search of victims until recent awareness of the problem forced changes in nursing homes' visitor policies.

The *modus operandi* is the same as it is for all those who exploit the elderly: cult workers approach elderly victims by using Wendy Lustbader's "three hungers." First, intimacy: they immediately call a person by first name, and they listen. They appear to care deeply when an older person opens up to them. Second, touch: gentle taking of the hand or light touches on the shoulder mean a lot to someone lacking simple touch in his or her life. Third, the need to be needed. "We need you," the cult workers will say, many times shouting the words. Along with the three hungers, answers to life's most complex questions are given in a soothing tone of voice.

Tragically, many older people get hooked into the most destructive cults. The most recent example is David Koresh's Branch Davidian cult, where many older retired people burned to death in Waco, Texas. It is hard to imagine an older couple going for a cult such as Koresh's in which all cult members' property and cash went to David Koresh, and even their wives were taken from them and given to him!

But what the rest of us must realize is how beautiful it seems in the beginning. In the beginning, nobody says, "We're all going to burn up together in Waco, Texas." In the beginning, if you join a cult, you are told that all your problems will be solved and that you will have no more worries. You are often told your health will improve dramatically. You are told that now you are part of a huge, loving family. You belong to something warm, huge, and loving. These promises are all appealing to older people facing the ends of their lives.

Like all other con artists, the cult workers and leaders work very hard to isolate victims from their old friends and families. This is very important to any con artist who wants to be successful. Brainwashing—and that is exactly what occurs in fanatical religions and cults—can occur only in isolated settings. The victims will only give them-

selves and their money over completely when they feel they have no-
where else to go. Hence the cult works to alienate the victims from
their families or from anyone who might care enough to separate
them from this destructive environment.

The saddest part of the process is that older people are isolated
from their families at the time in their lives when they most need to
be close to them. If you suspect that someone you love is being isolated by a fanatical religious group or a cult, you can contact the Cult
Awareness Network in Chicago, Illinois. Their telephone number is 1-
312-267-7777. Or you can contact your local Adult Protective Services
office and see what help they can offer you immediately.

For those looking for answers or comfort, the same warning we
gave against telemarketing and investment con artists holds true: "If
the promises sound too good to be true, they probably are." Don't believe them; at this writing, no one has found all the answers. If the
group making all these fabulous promises wants your money, do not
give it to them. You need it for yourself, for your comfortable old age.
If they want to see the title to your home—or even if they mention the
words "title" or "deed," call Adult Protective Services or the police.

If anyone tries to tell you your family is no good, or your adult
children are no good, your antennae should immediately rise. Why
would any decent person want you to be enemies with your own flesh
and blood? They wouldn't. Decent people want you to be close to
your flesh and blood at the end of your life, unless they are all hatchet
murderers or are abusing you badly. Decent people with no hidden
agenda would never try to take your petty family squabbles and turn
them into chasms that isolate you from your entire family.

Avoiding the Isolation
That Makes You Vulnerable

In all of the many cases of financial exploitation I've studied, the one
common factor is isolation. By isolation I mean that an older person
found himself or herself isolated from friends, family or society in
general. The reasons were various, but the result was always the same:
once a person is isolated from friends, family or society, a sociopath/
con artist knows he or she can move in and get close. The con artist

then goes right to work on the victim, isolating him or her further, and reality gets fuzzy: reality for the older victim becomes whatever reality the con artist creates. A successful con artist eliminates whatever small ties the victim may have had to family or friends, so the only social tie the victim has remaining is to that con artist. The victim then becomes completely dependent emotionally on the con artist. It is terribly easy in such a setting to drain every penny from a victim.

Isolation can occur gradually, for example when old neighborhood friends move away one by one and the new neighbors are of a completely different generation. Illness that gradually becomes disability can isolate a person as it becomes harder and harder to leave the house. The death of spouses and friends can result in isolation. At first, hit with severe loss and grief, a person stays in the house; to be alone and mourn freely feels comfortable at first, but gradually it grows harder and harder to return to society. Wendy Lustbader spoke of one client who told her, "Every morning after I get up, the bed calls to me." It can be hard to leave the home and the bed when depression and loss are at their worst.

Fortunately, there are many wonderful resources you can use now, before isolation sets in too badly. If you know you've already sunk into isolation, there are many ways to escape. The important thing is to reach out to good people and good resources before one of those con artists with the big computer lists contacts you. They are charming, lovely, friendly people and their allure is irresistible to a lonely soul.

The day you turned fifty, hopefully, you joined AARP. I cannot believe how much AARP has to offer: amazing discounts on credit cards, health insurance, automobile insurance, free publications about career changes, and free financial advice. They offer job-hunting seminars through their AARP Works program, and a specialized Woman's Financial Network. You also get the magazine, *Modern Maturity*, which will keep you abreast of everything from scams to avoid, to great things—as well as bad—happening for older Americans in Washington. All this for only $8.00! If you haven't yet joined, and you're over fifty, contact AARP, P.O. Box 199, Long Beach, CA, 90801.

Another group to join is the Gray Panthers, whose slogan is "Age and Youth in Action." As Maggie Kuhn, the founder of Gray Panthers, said, "Speak your mind—even if your voice shakes. Well-aimed slingshots can topple giants." Gray Panthers get involved, and nothing is so exhilarating as fighting a good fight for what is right. Some of the Panthers' good fights have been universal health care, age discrimination, economic and tax justice, affordable housing, and world peace. To learn more, contact the Gray Panthers, 2025 Pennsylvania Avenue NW, Suite 821, Washington, DC, 20006.

There are many wonderful groups to join, and most local papers list the times and locations different groups meet. You'll be amazed, if you've never looked at how many different groups there are—from widow support groups and Alzheimer support groups, to bird-watching, handicrafts and wine-tasting groups. No matter what your interests, ability, or energy level, there is a group for you to join. For example, in Pagosa Springs, Colorado, the Gray Wolves meet weekly in the summer to hike the glorious Rockies. You can climb cliffs with the most robust Gray Wolves, or you can wheel your wheelchair down a serene asphalt path with the physically challenged Gray Wolves. There are levels for everyone in the Gray Wolves, and I've never met more fun people in one place than I have at a Gray Wolves meeting. (My husband was even made an honorary member because his beard was prematurely gray.) Along the same lines, you can join the Sierra Club, which has chapters all over the country. Whether hiking or birdwatching, they are always doing something interesting. One paraplegic friend, for example, went river rafting with the Sierra Club. Look in your local telephone book to get the local chapter's number, and ask for a free brochure or newsletter. The official headquarters of the Sierra Club is 730 Polk Street, San Francisco, CA 94109.

A great way to get yourself motivated to exercise is to take a class. The YMCA and YWCA offer tremendous exercise programs for every age and ability at rock-bottom prices. Look in your local phone book for the YMCA or YWCA nearest you, and call to ask for a free schedule of classes. I watched a YWCA water-exercise class for disabled elderly men and women, and it was a joy to watch. In the water, after all, we are all freer, and the faces on the people doing the simple exercises were happy. They could move, and they were laughing together. If you don't have a "Y" near you, you probably have a county-run recreation center. Look in the "County Government" pages of your phone book and call the recreation center to get a free schedule of their classes. They are often very reasonably priced, with discounts for seniors.

If you call your local junior college, they will send you a free schedule of the classes they are offering. College, you will notice immediately, ain't what it used to be! There are classes for every imaginable interest: square dancing offered by the P.E. department, or ceramics and painting from the art department, and "grief" classes from the psychology department. Read the whole schedule to get creative ideas. Seniors, of course, get terrific discounts on tuition.

If you belong to a church or temple, you may not have noticed that there are many temple- and church-organized activities. You may have been too busy in the past, working or tending a family, to even read the weekly bulletins. Now may be the time to sign up for some of these activities and get more acquainted with some of the people you've been sitting with so many Saturdays or Sundays.

If you find yourself isolated because you're caring for a spouse or parent with Alzheimer's or some other disease, there are havens available for you. Known as adult day care centers, these are bright, cheery places you can drop off your loved one. Your spouse or parent will receive stimulation, while you get a break—maybe to take a class or join a group. (Yes, you're exhausted, but doing something fun with other people will pep you up and do more good for you than doing chores or napping.) Look in your local yellow pages for adult day care centers, or call your local senior center, or look in your local county government section for your local Area Agency on Aging to find out what adult day care is available in your area. Ask the center what discounts you are eligible for. Most ADCs try to be reasonably priced, and the best thing is that your spouse or parent tends to come home happier than when you left them.

Another option along those lines—giving you, the caretaker, "space"—is Kelly Assisted Living, or some other part-time in-home help. Kelly Assisted Living is operated by the same people who run the Kelly temporary office help business, with the similar idea of a temporary worker who comes and goes as you need her or him. You can call 1-800-YES-KELLY to get more information.

Sign up for more than you think you can manage. That way if one class turns out not to be for you, you won't end up sitting home crabby. Try many groups and classes until you find the right ones. You will find yourself less vulnerable, busy, and having a much better time than if you stayed home watching TV.

Financial Abuse by Family Members

Mary's Story

Mary had the most beautiful eyes I had ever seen. They were jade green. In China, that color jade is known as apple-green jade. Her eyes were clear, and pierced through me. She was eighty-four years old. Looking into those eyes, I began to realize the depths of her pain. It was not about the money. Her vulnerability was palpable, and it hurt to be there with her; but in addition to that vulnerability, which made her tremble like a wounded, cornered animal, there was also the explosive force of a volcano as she spoke.

"I trusted my son!" she shouted at me. There was no quiver in her voice, and her ancient hand grabbed mine fiercely. "Everybody wants to know, 'How could you let this happen, let him take everything over so many years? What's the matter with you—are you senile, you old broad?' That's what they're thinking, but does anyone ever believe their own son is going to take his mother's house and all her millions of dollars? People tried to warn me about him, but he was my own son. I would not listen to anything evil said about my own son. I nursed him at my own breast," she shouted, pounding herself there. "And now he's dead to me. I've lost a son."

Her eyes filled with water, but no tears fell, and her piercing stare that stabbed into me never wavered. The grip she had on my hand tightened and grew stronger. I had to ask her about the things she signed, because not all of the papers transferring her properties from herself to her son were forged. She sighed from the bottom of her soul—the kind of sigh you only sigh when you've lived a very long time.

She looked away, as if viewing the incident. "No, I didn't read everything. He'd rush in, give me some line about what a rush he was in or how he was going to make me lots of money in a big new deal, and he needed my signature right away." The beautiful eyes returned to me. "I trusted my son," she said, quietly this time. She was exhausted, and I suggested she might like to rest.

"Oh hell, no. Let's go have some fun and drop this dreary stuff."

Eve's Story

It was clear she was in a great deal of pain; she held her hip at an odd angle, as if to take the pressure off of it. Her fingers were gnarled from arthritis, and her back was hunched over from osteoporosis, but her eyes danced like the eyes of a young girl. She told me she wanted her "fake name" to be Eve, "because Eve is a sexy name for a dame, and I may not look like a sexy dame to you, but that's what I am to me, inside here." She tenderly pointed to her heart.

Eve now lives in the Pacific Northwest, but she has lived all over the United States and Cuba. As she wove her tale, her Texas accent grew stronger. "My daughter," she laughed, lighting a cigarette. "In Texas, we call her kind a 'fart blossom.' She's been married eight times, and she's been in jail three times. Know what for? Shopliftin', of all things! Lord. Let me tell you somethin', honey. In this world, there's givers and there's takers, and she is one fart blossom taker. She went into my car when I was movin' into this here one-story house, on account of my hip made me leave the big ol' three-story house I was livin' in down south. Little fart blossom, she went into a big sack where I'd put the deed to property my daddy gave me upon his passin'. Property in Texas, California, Louisiana—Lord, just name a place. It's all gone. And I got a son who's as good as they come, and I got so many friends I could drive the northern route across this country, come back the southern route, and never once stay in a hotel. These are the good people I want to leave my things to when I go. I was pretty depressed, you know, when I found out. But I never stay down too long."

She watched clouds gathering together overhead, and with a sweep of her hand bid me to do the same. A storm is coming, I think. "What, you think it's gonna' rain?" she asked me, reading my thoughts. I smiled, but she continued before I could say a word. "Not a chance. Just cloudin' up for nothin'. Hard for me to get used to, when I come from a place where weatha' was weatha'. Sky'd by a perfect blue, then you blink your eyes twice, and black clouds'd be everywhere. Within ten minutes, thunda'd be bustin' your eardrums, and you'd look like a soaked cat.

"Thing is, I'm a worker. Worked all my life—in the cemetery business, now there's a business that's good in every economy!—and I can't understand the takers who just want to come along and take, do no work at all. Can you imagine? So I make some phone calls, and I find out that since I don't have the deeds to the property—she has 'em—that I maybe don't own 'em anymore. I went through the roof when I heard that! And the person on the phone doesn't care, they just sittin' there silent on the phone. Maybe thinkin', 'Who cares about this old dame?' But you listen, honey, and you get this down." She smoked while I wrote, waiting and watching to be sure I wrote every word. "This sexy dame with the bad hip and ugly old face is not long for this world, but my last breath is gonna' be a fightin' one. Fart Blossom is not gettin' away with this, and you're a honeybunch for helpin' me. Write that down."

I did, and then I called the Adult Protective Services supervisor in her area. APS would get Eve in touch with lawyers and a variety of systems in the other states that would get her property titles transferred back into her name. The daughter, we discovered, had transferred the titles from her mother's to her name through forgeries.

Eve was very happy to hear all this. "Thank God," she said when I told her.

Sofia's Story

Sofia (not her real name) is from Egypt, but she has lived in the U.S. most of her adult life. She is short and round, with black hair and large, expressive black eyes. Her accent is rich, reminding me of ancient deserts and fabled cities buried in the sand. Hers is a tradition of harsh repression of women—she is Moslem—yet whenever I meet women from countries where women are hidden behind veils, I am always amazed by their inner strengths. Sofia is no different.

Her complexion is that of a young woman, smooth and honey-colored, but the pain she has suffered is easy to read in her large black eyes. Still, she smiled with great dignity when I handed her a cup of thick, sweet coffee.

"This is coffee from my country," she said, smiling, and her face grew girlish before my eyes. I asked her when her last trip home to Egypt had been, and she said, "Ten years ago, just before my husband died. We went to bury his brother." Her head was down as she remembered.

Sofia and her husband—in America, "everybody called him Mike"—came to America when she was pregnant with their first son. Mike had cousins in Boston who had become very prosperous as taxi drivers; they now owned their own taxi company, and had invited

Mike to work for them.

"It was so strange, being in this huge place. I was very frightened, but we had a big family around us, and we wore the same clothes as we did at home. We never spoke English, and we ate the same food as in Egypt, so nothing was different. Life for Egyptian women was exactly the same."

In Egypt, a woman is considered the property of a man. She obeys him and depends on him for everything. The world outside the walls of home is considered evil and treacherous, so the woman remains behind the walls of her home. In Sofia's culture, it is unthinkable for a woman to work outside the home. Her duty is to cook, clean, and rear the children. Sofia has four children, two boys and two girls.

"They came very quickly, boom, boom," she said, and smiled another girlish smile that was both shy and proud. Mike had been proud of the children, but he had to work eighteen hours a day driving a taxi to support his family. "He was so stubborn," Sofia said. "I told him, 'I can sew for money in my house while the children are sleeping,' but he would not hear of it. 'No wife of mine will work for money,' he said. So he worked more, driving sometimes twenty hours a day."

They moved to another large American city where taxi drivers made a better living, and Sofia felt lost without the huge network of her husband's family. Because she rarely went outside the home except to shop, she remained completely isolated. Her life was her children, and she lived for their return from school, when she could breathe in the exotic air of knowledge.

"I was so glad they made all the children go to school. My husband tried to fight and keep the girls home, but the Americans said, 'You live in America, so follow American laws, and school is the law.' I was so happy for my girls. They were very smart, eager learners. You know, my oldest girl, Lydia, she is a doctor now. A good doctor, a pediatrician."

Although it was Sofia's job to budget the money for groceries and clothing—most of which she sewed herself—she knew absolutely nothing about how her husband was investing their money, or even how much money there was. He had acquired several taxis, and he worked constantly. They lived in a lovely neighborhood, but the family never saw Mike. By the time he came home at night, the children were in bed. Often he left while they were still asleep, or sometimes he would catch up on desperately needed sleep, and the children would leave quietly for school in the morning without seeing him.

When he was around, on Sunday, Mike was crabby and stern. "He ruled like a mean tyrant king," Sofia said, making a fist, but not without pride. (I was surprised by this.) "He never hit anybody, but he was always shouting, slamming his fist. The children were so afraid of him. He was just like my father, so I was used to it. They spent all their time with me, and I am quiet. They never grew used to him."

When Ron, their oldest son, showed no promise at school, Mike decided he would follow his country's tradition and give Ron the taxi business. (The other three children did very well in school, and became a doctor, a lawyer, and a college professor.) With Ron taking over much of the driving, Mike, in his later years, finally got some rest. Father and son worked hard together, and their company grew.

"Ron was just like his father in every way, except he had no heart. Mike had a heart, a big heart, about everything. Ron was always like a machine," Sofia said sadly.

At the age of fifty-four, Mike was gunned down in his taxi in the middle of a Saturday night. Sofia said, "I couldn't believe it. This man who was my life, who told me every little thing to do, was gone. The only thing to do was go on with my life as always, with Ron doing the business, taking charge."

The taxi business was considerable, and for a while everything ran smoothly. But Sofia and Ron started to fight about money. There never seemed to be enough. "Mike always gave me whatever I asked for, but Ron was very stingy with me and his wife."

One day Ron came and told Sofia the house was for sale, "and it was like a knife in my heart," Sofia said. When the house was sold, the money paid off debts. Ron informed Sofia there was nothing left, and she was left homeless.

"I know Mike never thought his son would do this to his mother," Sofia said. Fortunately, she was able to move in with Lydia, her oldest daughter, and her family. She now lives in a small guest house in the back, and watches Lydia's small children while Lydia is at work.

The entire family was shocked to learn that Ron's problem was cocaine. "Drugs!" Sofia spat out the word that has destroyed her life. She was shocked to learn that Ron had gone through four million dollars in ten years without anyone knowing a thing. "We never dreamed there was so much money, or that Ron was taking drugs," Sofia said. (Ron is now in jail, for cocaine possession and trafficking.) "My God, my poor husband, he worked so hard to make that much money; how badly he must be feeling, wherever he is."

She sighed and said, "At least I know my daughters will never have this problem. Thank God for America giving women the right to know everything and to work for themselves and their families. It is better this way."

Sofia has begun to earn some money of her own, through her beautiful sewing. She is proud of her work and the income it brings, and she is happy caring for her grandchildren. She is luckier than many woman who have been robbed by their own children. She will be okay.

Financial Abuse by Other Family Members

It is very hard to imagine our beautiful babies growing up to steal all our money and our assets, but it happens at an alarming rate throughout the country. At the moment it is difficult to get precise figures; it's as if the crime is so horrible that no one wants to quantify it. I've spoken with one champion of elder fiduciary rights who says that 29% of all financial abuse of elders is committed by the victims' grown children. However, Toshio Tatara, who is one of the country's most authoritative data collectors on elder abuse, disputes that 29%, saying that 29% of all types of abuse against the elderly is perpetrated by their offspring. He says there hasn't been a breakdown of how much *financial* abuse against the elderly is perpetrated by the offspring. When I said, "But in all the cases I've heard, it does seem to work out that about one third of the financial exploitation is perpetrated by offspring." He said, "Maybe so. We don't know the figure yet."

Whatever the exact percentage, law enforcement officers trained to investigate financial elder abuse cases all over the country told me that financial abuse by family members—usually the offspring of the victims—is increasingly common. Looking through the 1994 reports from each state on financial exploitation, the wealthiest counties get the largest numbers of financial exploitation reports. This suggests that if you're rich, you're in the gravest danger. According to Adult Protective Services workers from every state, however, the most common complaint is adult children stealing their parents' Social Security checks. Rich or poor, when sons and daughters decide to rob their parents, they usually don't stop until they've taken it all.

"We get an awful lot of those complaints," the APS workers all said, referring to sons and daughters taking their parents' money. And they all agreed that the most maddening thing about this type of crime is how difficult it is to prosecute. Unfortunately, after speaking with both law enforcement officers and Adult Protective Services workers across the nation, I've come to the grim realization that this heartbreaking form of financial abuse is nearly impossible to prosecute.

According to Paul Cirincione, an APS specialist for Broward County, Florida, most financial abuse of the elderly perpetrated by family members goes unprosecuted in Florida. He says it will continue to go unprosecuted, "until incompetence proceedings improve across the board." Right now, he says, the problem with financial exploitation is the assumption that the victims have full mental capacity unless the courts decide they're incompetent.

"It is hard to prove the victim's mental state was impaired at the time he or she wrote away their estate," Cirincione says. "The defense will always come back with, 'She was perfectly fine at the time, and she wanted to give her home and all her money to her son.' It's very difficult to prove the elder person was tricked or taken advantage of, and in Florida we won't even try. Who's to say she wasn't fully competent and just stupidly gave it away? Now, we are successful when the elderly person formally asks for financial help, and the 'helper' clearly abuses that position as helper. Florida's laws surrounding exploitation require that I use *your* money for *me* in order for exploitation to exist. A son writing checks on his mother's account, for example, could stretch the truth drastically to say his mother benefitted from every single check he wrote. If he's a good talker, no action will be taken.

"The other problem," Cirincione continued, "is the relationship that often exists between the victim and the perpetrator. The victim wants to protect the perpetrator. We can never get victims to do it, to send their own kids to prison. In domestic violence cases, on the other hand, the victim does not need to testify at all. Many changes in legislation must be made before these elderly-exploitation cases can be successfully prosecuted, and they will be made. We're working on these legislative changes right now in Florida."

It is very hard to guess whether or not your adult children will come after your money. In "Elder Abuse in the United States: An Issue Paper," (Toshio Tatara, Director, NARCEA, 1990), Dr. Tatara states that adult children who abuse their elderly parents suffer from such problems as mental and emotional disorders, alcoholism, drug addiction, or financial difficulty. Often, adult children who have these problems are dependent upon their parents, whom they abuse. The parents feel guilty for "failing" to raise successful, healthy children, and do not report the abuse until the situation is quite desperate.

If you have adult children with any of these problems, it is urgently important for you to establish a living trust, and put all of your assets and real estate into it. If the troubled adult child has to go to a trust officer every time he or she wants money, and if the trust officer refuses, the adult child may be forced to face his or her problems without depleting you. If your home is your only asset, it's worth putting it in a living trust. If a Social Security check is your only source of income, it is very easy to establish a "direct deposit" system, whereby checks are mailed directly to your bank account, and cannot be stolen. Talk to your bank about using this service.

If you have a troubled adult child and you have a brokerage account, establish a "password security system" with them, whereby they will not say one word to anyone about your account without a password. Make the password something so personal that you could never forget it, and no one else could ever guess it.

If you have a troubled adult child, never let them near your finances. Never give them power of attorney under any circumstances; they could absolutely wipe you out with it. Use a living trust instead. Remember, a general power of attorney gives absolute and complete power to whomever you give it to. Avoid it!

I have heard thousands of case histories about ruthless adult offspring stealing their elderly parents' money. In "Mary's Story," above, her son decimated the $20-million estate her husband had left her and her other six children. At this writing, Mary is still in her home, but the son has taken so many loans on her home that it is doubtful she can remain. Her cash supply is dwindling rapidly, as she must make payments on those loans. Amazingly, her son is not in jail, although it can be proven that he grossly abused his mother's fiduciary trust. She trusted her son, and our current laws somehow do not allow for these types of white-collar criminals to be punished.

According to A. Paul Blunt, an attorney in Arizona specializing in financial abuse of the elderly, trust is the common denominator in most of these cases. Because of lack of financial knowledge, diminished capacity, or grief, elderly victims place complete trust in persons—in these cases adult children—who use that trust to rob them.

As with all other forms of elderly exploitation, the "bad" son or daughter works to completely isolate the parent. Terrible lies are spread by the perpetrator against other offspring, who might investigate their financial activities and rescue the parent. Often, the perpetrator will say, "Mom, I'm your only friend. The others all want to put you in a home."

Again, isolation is the most dangerous enemy of the elderly. If you are an adult child who has been shunned by an elderly parent in favor of a sibling, do not withdraw. No matter how hurt you feel by your mom's or dad's rejection, keep all lines of communication open. Your parent may be asking you to withdraw because he or she is being brainwashed or threatened. It is time to get suspicious; the more you are asked to withdraw, the more you should investigate. Carefully read the chapter "Abuse Signals: How to Spot Probable Abuse," and act!

Wendy Lustbader, M.S.W., Lectures on Financial Abuse by Family Members

Wendy Lustbader, of the Pike Market Medical Clinic in Seattle, has counseled countless elderly clients whose adult children and grandchildren have abused them. More than anyone I've spoken with, Ms. Lustbader seems to have a firm grasp of both the enormity and the origins of the problem, and her insights are valuable.

According to the 1990 census, 3.2 million children were living with their grandparents. That is a 40% increase from the 1980 figures, but Ms. Lustbader feels strongly that this figure is still too low. She expects the numbers to vastly increase when the next census is taken. These figures are directly connected to the following tragic statistic:

11% of all children born in the United States are exposed to drugs prenatally—primarily to cocaine. Sadly, drug- and alcohol-dependent adult children are giving their babies to their parents to raise. In other cases, grandparents who have given up on their drug- or alcohol-dependent adult children are taking their grandchildren into their homes to save those kids.

In a lecture presented to APS workers from all over the country, Lustbader told heartbreaking stories of older women clients of hers, saying she hears these types of stories frequently. The stories all begin with a client's appearance deteriorating so rapidly that she investigates and discovers that the client's adult child, spouse, and grandchildren have moved in with the client. The couple turns out to be drug or alcohol dependent, and are using the client's Social Security checks to buy liquor or drugs. The client, having a medical condition requiring medication, can no longer afford to buy medicine once the family has moved in. Lustbader tries to reason with these clients—mostly women—telling them they are doing great harm to themselves by letting these troubled families live with them. She suggests these women tell the families to live elsewhere.

The response is very often the same: "That little grandchild is the light of my life!" The loving grandmas absolutely refuse to abandon the innocent grandchildren. The drug- or alcohol-dependent adult child knows this, and threatens the parent when the Social Security check is not forthcoming. The parent is either threatened with physical harm or, most effectively, the adult child threatens to take away the grandchild. The threats work, and the parent is terrorized into handing over his or her check. Lustbader must remind these grandmothers that they won't be much good to their grandchildren dead. They need to take care of themselves in order to help their grandchildren.

It is common for these older parents to feel guilt and shame, Lustbader says. Some of them feel they deserve the abuse they're getting from their adult children, because they were not good parents.

"When I come into these situations, I'm always intersecting a human life in the middle of a story. Often there is a legacy of hatred and abuse." Lustbader's goal is to stop the cycle of abuse, which sometimes spans many generations. "You may have made mistakes as a parent," she says to them, "but that doesn't mean you deserve this abuse."

Lustbader is very clear about solutions to this kind of elderly abuse. She believes in practicing "tough love" with adult children. She believes you should deny them the money they demand, notify authorities, or do whatever it takes to get the adult child into a drug or alcohol rehabilitation program. She believes above all that you should put your money out of reach. With Social Security checks, for example, you can talk to your bank about "direct deposit," as mentioned above. Or you can designate a trusted friend to be your "protective payee." A protective payee will receive your checks for you and will immediately purchase necessary medicine and food supplies for your home. He or she can pay your necessary bills as well, so that your heating isn't turned off, for example.

In these complicated mutli-generational situations, it is vitally important, says Lustbader, that Adult Protective Services, Child Protective Services, and alcohol and drug rehabilitation systems all connect with each other. They must coordinate their efforts, interact, and work jointly every step of the way to solve a family's problems.

AFDC (Aid to Families with Dependent Children) rules must change as well, according to Lustbader. At the moment, for example, it is often difficult to transfer AFDC benefits from the child's parents to the grandparents, even though the grandparents are solely responsible for the child. Likewise, foster parent regulations must change. For example, regulations currently stipulate that foster parents' homes must have a certain number of rooms; in some situations, grandparents are so fearful of discovery that they are hiding their grandchildren in the senior housing apartments. They're afraid of their troubled adult children, and they're afraid of losing the small benefits they get from foster parent programs or AFDC—all of which go to caring for these children. They shouldn't have to live this way.

The greatest help of all for these beleaguered grandparents, says Lustbader, is grandparent support groups. In the appendix "Resources" you'll find several of these listed.

Preventing Elder Abuse

Abuse Signals:
How to Spot Financial Abuse of an Elder

MARY JOY QUINN, the Court Investigator for San Francisco's Superior Court, compiled the following list of indicators of financial abuse. It was included in *Elder Abuse and Neglect: Causes, Diagnosis and Intervention by Quinn and Tomita.* If you have noticed any of these indicators in a relative or close friend of yours, you should contact the Adult Protective Services office in your area.

1. There is unusual or inappropriate activity in the older person's bank accounts. Example: accounts changed from one branch of a bank to another, or drastic changes in types and amounts of withdrawals and transactions being made, despite the fact that the elder cannot get to the bank due to illness or impairment.

2. Bank statements and cancelled checks no longer come to the elder's home.

3. Documents are constantly being drawn up for the elder's signature, but the elder cannot understand what they mean. Examples might include power of attorney, a will, joint tenancy on a bank account, or a deed to the house. The elder may say he or she has been signing papers but doesn't remember what they were.

4. The care of the elder is not commensurate with the size of the estate. A caregiver may refuse to spend money on the care of the elder. There may be numerous unpaid bills such as overdue rent, utilities, or taxes, when someone is supposed to be in charge of the elder's money. There may be a lack of amenities (personal grooming or appropriate clothing) even though the older person's estate can well af-

165

ford them.

5. The primary caregiver expresses unusual interest in the amount of money being expended on the care of the elder and asks too many financial questions.

6. Recent acquaintances express gushy, undying affection for a wealthy older person.

7. Personal belongings are missing, such as art, silverware, jewelry, or furs.

8. The elder appears isolated from family or friends. For example, a housekeeper may try to isolate the older person from other family members by claiming that they do not care about him or her. The housekeeper then tells the family that the elder does not want to see them, and later induces the elder to sign over assets by claiming to be the only person who cares about him or her.

9. A caregiver or recent acquaintance makes promises of lifelong care for the elder—for example, "I'll keep you out of a nursing home"—in exchange for money or property.

10. Signatures on checks or other documents appear suspicious. The signature may not resemble the older person's handwriting, or there may be "signatures" on documents or checks even though the older person cannot write.

11. There is a lack of solid documentation or formal arrangements for financial management of the elder. In these cases, the primary caregiver may attempt to evade questions about the sources of income.

12. There are implausible explanations about the finances of the elder by the caregiver and/or the elder.

13. The elder is unaware of or does not understand financial arrangements that have been made. For example, an eviction notice arrives when the elder thought she or he owned the house.

If any of these have occurred, you can take the following measures:

1. Demand that an attorney or accountant review all of the elder's financial accounts.

2. Require two signatures on all accounts.

3. Set up periodic meetings to review the financial records.

4. Check the deeds to all of the elder's real property with the

County Recorder's office to see if any transfers have been made.

5. Find out if any power of attorney documents have been signed. Ask the elder's bank, brokerage firm, and the County Recorder's office about deeds, titles, etc. If a power of attorney has been signed, see an attorney about getting it annulled.

6. Find out whether any joint tenancy accounts have been established on bank accounts, brokerage accounts, or deeds to property. Get them cancelled.

7. Even if there's been no alteration such as power of attorney or joint tenancy established, if you are suspicious, call the elder's bank and tell them to "flag" the elder's account so that it will be observed with more caution.

8. If an account has been misused—for example, if suspicious checks have been written—close the account and open a new one requiring two signatures.

9. Request copies of cancelled checks, bank statements, and withdrawals.

10. If forgery or misuse of funds is apparent, the client can sign an affidavit with the bank and it will be investigated. The police or FBI may get involved.

Avoiding Problems Early: The Living Trust

Everyone over forty should consider establishing a "revocable living trust." A revocable living trust is a legal document used to plan and organize your estate. The document spells out the explicit, detailed desires of its creator concerning all his or her assets. "Living" means the trust was created and is effective while you are living. "Revocable" means it can be changed or cancelled while you're alive.

The person or persons who create the trust can act as their own trustees, so there are no management fees or loss of control. (Or you can designate the person of your choice to manage the trust.) A revocable living trust can be changed at any time until the creator of the trust—the trustor—dies. Then the living trust becomes "irrevocable."

There are many reasons why a living trust is essential to Americans over fifty-five. First, because we are living so much longer than ever before, we must be prepared for the reality that many of us will become incapacitated before we die. For that matter, a car accident could incapacitate us in our prime! In your living trust you will state whom you wish to govern your financial affairs should you become incompetent.

By using a living trust you will avoid being placed under public guardianship. Investigative reporters in Florida uncovered a huge scandal surrounding court-appointed public guardians. Apparently some of them had criminal records before their appointments, and they were grossly abusing their elderly clients financially.

Another tragic example of what can happen without a living trust is the Groucho Marx case. The last three years of Groucho Marx's life were a nightmare; he was infirm, and had to attend many probate court hearings. Because the court declared him incompetent—a declaration he greatly resented—he had no say whatsoever in the proceedings. Reports of the trials were that Mr. Marx would sit crying while his relatives and the woman he'd lived with for many years fought over his estate. Because of the fighting, every detail of Mr. Marx's lifestyle and habits were dragged into the very public trial. What must have been three years of living hell for all concerned would have been completely avoided had Marx established a living trust. He would have stated whom he wanted to run his financial affairs and how, should he be declared incompetent.

Most married couples place their real estate and stocks in "joint tenancy, with right of survivorship." A living trust is actually a better way to go. If your home or stocks are in joint tenancy and your spouse has a stroke or becomes incompetent, you will not be able to sell them. You will have to first get the probate court to declare your spouse incompetent, and then the court must appoint you the conservator. You will then have to keep very scrupulous records in order to satisfy the court which will want to meet with you frequently. All probate court proceedings are public record.

Instead of holding your real estate in joint tenancy, hold it in a living trust. The title would read, "Joe and Mary Smith, trustees of the Joe and Mary Smith revocable living trust." Total control over your real estate remains with you. If both of you were to die simultaneously, your living trust would designate who the beneficiary was to be. This is not the case with joint tenancy where, if both joint tenants die simultaneously, the court decides who will be the beneficiary.

Most people use the revocable living trust to avoid probate, and to save money on estate taxes for their heirs. Probate is a mandatory public process in which a person's estate is placed into the court system. Assets are frozen; beneficiaries cannot get to the assets for anywhere from four months to two years. A revocable living trust completely eliminates that process, along with its many costs and fees. Assets go immediately to beneficiaries, and it's all done very privately. Unlike wills, which can be very easily contested, it is very difficult to contest a living trust, and almost nobody who has tried has succeeded.

Current federal estate tax law states that $600,000 of your assets will be excluded from federal estate tax. With a revocable living trust, however, you can pass up to $1.2 million tax-free to your heirs.

Because living trusts have become so popular, there is a great deal of competition in the estate services business. Take advantage of this competition and shop around; it is very important that you do not attempt to create your own living trust. There are books available that contain the forms, and they give pretty good instructions, but there is too great a risk when you make your own trust. Just by using the wrong form or signing in the wrong place, you could completely invalidate the trust. Get a qualified attorney to write up your living trust; it is worth the extra money to have it done correctly.

A common complaint regarding living trusts is the hassle of getting all your real estate and securities titles transferred into the living trust. It is no longer such a problem, however. Living trusts have become so common that most estate services give you one easy form to fill out for each large asset (small checking accounts and cars don't usually go into living trusts), and they do the rest. They contact your mutual fund company and get real estate titles transferred quickly, easily, and privately. For income tax purposes, during your lifetime the trust uses your social security number(s). All income from the trust can be reported on IRS form 1040.

Another advantage a living trust has over a will is that all real property throughout the country is covered. Without a living trust you might have to go through probate with a different attorney in each state in which you own property. This multiple-probate process would rack up enormous fees that could be completely avoided.

Probate fees can vary so widely that they are hard to estimate; but the AARP did a 1990 study on probate costs and concluded that they can run from ten to twenty percent of the entire estate. That is a terrible waste of money when you can so easily avoid it. On the other hand, to establish a living trust should only cost from $700 to an absolute maximum of $1,800 (for the largest, most complicated estates). $1,000 is the common "going rate."

Robert Esperti and Renno Peterson are lawyers and authors who have written many books on living trusts. *Loving Trust* (Viking, 1994) is their most recent book on the subject. In it they compare the living trust to the detailed, gummy-stickered notes you leave all over the house when you hire a babysitter to watch your children. Nothing is left to chance when you leave your children in the babysitter's care; every conceivable emergency is anticipated. With the living trust it is the same.

For example, if you have children or grandchildren in your care who are minors, you'll name the person whom you want to act as guardian in case something happens to you. (Make sure the guardians have agreed to this before you name them.) You will also stipulate at what age you wish a minor to inherit certain monies. For example, a forty-one-year-old attorney I spoke with told me he'd created a living trust whereby his brother would become his five-year-old daughter's guardian, should he die. He named his bank as the financial manager of the trust, however, with stipulations that his daughter would get only so much money on her eighteenth birthday, so much at college graduation, and the rest on her thirtieth birthday.

Before setting up an appointment with a qualified attorney to establish your living trust, you or you and your spouse should sit down and make decisions about whom you want to manage things. If you have several adult children, you can name all of them co-successors to the trust in the event of your demise. You can also name your bank, and you can meet with the department of your bank that deals with trusts and estate management to work out the details.

Keep an eye on your local newspaper for free seminars on estate planning. These are often presented by estate preparation services or estate attorneys. Use caution, however, and don't let anyone at the seminar pressure you into anything. You are there solely for free information; you owe them nothing. Take your information and go home to mull over what you have learned. As in any other situation, anyone who tries to rush you into something—anything—should be suspect.

I attended a free estate planning seminar presented by Don Woods, one of the founders of Kensington Estate Services, which has offices in seventeen states. I asked him to briefly describe the process of setting up a living trust, which he did.

On your initial visit with an estate lawyer, he or she will go over all the bases you may wish to cover in your living trust. You will spend a good three hours, probably, discussing all of your desires, so make sure you've jotted down all the things you want to discuss. When you make your appointment, you may be instructed to bring real estate deeds and stock certificates.

Your visit will get personal, perhaps, when you discuss certain fore-seeable problems in your complex family situation, but you must discuss them. You are trying to protect yourself with the living trust, so you must consider all possible catastrophes in order to prevent your own devastation. When this lengthy initial consultation is over, you will be sent home with instructions and forms to fill out. Your attorney will do everything else.

Because the living trust has become so popular, scams have recently appeared, as could be predicted. Beware of anyone approaching you out of the blue to establish a living trust. Like a good contractor, a good estate lawyer doesn't need to go out to hustle business. Beware of living trust kits sold through magazines, television ads, mailers, and door-to-door salespeople. A document this important should only be drawn up by a qualified attorney. Also beware of phoney promoters who charge a fee to learn about your financial information under the guise of drafting the trust. They may be con artists getting that information for their giant suckers list. Also be careful when choosing the establishment to draw up your living trust. Make sure it is a known and reputable organization, and not one that simply sounds like a well-known organization.

Before choosing the lawyer or estate service to draft this essential document, check with your local senior law center. You can get the number of your state's Agency on Aging, located at the back of this book, and ask them for the senior law center nearest you. Ask the staff at your senior law center if they recommend a certain establishment for drawing up living trusts, or ask if the lawyers or establishments you're thinking of approaching are reputable. Ask if they know of any complaints, and what those complaints are.

Living Trusts for Everyone Over Forty: Donna Shahan, Estate Lawyer

Donna Shahan is an attorney specializing in trust and probate law. She once worked in a private firm drawing up trusts, but she now works for Kensington Estate Services. Shahan says that Kensington's size and its presence in seventeen states was part of her reason for joining the firm.

"I like the idea that my clients don't have to worry about this company not being around to help their heirs after their deaths. Also, if something does go wrong, Kensington has the resources to set everything right." (Meaning that if they screw up, you can sue them.)

I told Shahan about some of the cases I'd been studying, cases involving both crooked adult children and bereft spouses who had been fleeced by con artists, and she had some great ideas about things people can do while they're still "up and running," as she put it.

"First, any parent or spouse can get a lawyer to draw up a durable power of attorney. While you are healthy and alert, you pick who will have power of attorney if something happens. It takes the opinions of two physicians to determine whether or not a person is fully capable, so an adult child can't just slip himself into a power of attorney. Durable power of attorney documents for both financial and health matters are an important part of any overall estate plan. The most important thing a durable power of attorney does is avoid conservatorship, should one spouse become incapacitated. The person chosen by you will manage affairs if you lose it, so you'd better choose someone reliable!"

She and I laughed; that can be difficult! But give yourself plenty of time when you or you and your spouse are alone and healthy. Go over everyone you know. You're bound to agree eventually on the most honest person you know. If you don't trust anyone, pick a professional who is impartial and who's big enough to be sued if something goes wrong.

Shahan had a lot more to say about trusts and durable power of attorney. "A durable power of attorney for health is important because you can tell whoever you've left in charge that you don't want your life to be prolonged artificially. If you become incapacitated, your health will be taken care of exactly the way you want it to be done."

"Can you tell me about your own living trust?" I asked.

"Yes. I drew up a revocable living trust for my son, even though I'm only forty. In the living trust I drew up for him, I stipulated that he doesn't get squat until he graduates from college, and then he gets half at twenty-five and half at thirty. I don't know what you were like at twenty-five, but I know what I was like, and he's got my blood in him! This estate service company is only getting bigger, so I know they'll be around after I kick off, and all their services from now until I die are free. I'm real happy with it.

"The money you save your kids by creating a trust instead of a will is incredible. If a couple had a so-called A-B living trust, with separate trusts for the husband and wife, they can pass up to $1.2 million tax-free to their children. Without the A-B living trust, the kids would pay $235,000 just in federal estate taxes on $1.2 million, and that's not even counting attorney's fees. And the property thing: so many older people put their property and financial accounts into joint tenancy with their rotten kids—or any damned con artist that talks them into it or tricks them. These slimes then get equal access to the accounts. They can control what happens to that property or account. It's a terrible mistake! Absolutely all of it should go into a living trust with careful stipulations. Lock it up and keep it safe.

"A lot of smart parents make all their kids 'co-successor trustees' to administer the trust according to their spelled-out wishes. If all the kids do it together, one can't accuse the other of anything. It's a good plan." She laughed. "Let's face it, it's not a perfect world, and we are not perfect people; but if you protect yourself, you'll be a whole lot happier."

Solutions: Views from Adult Protective Services Supervisors

For this chapter I have interviewed Adult Protective Services supervisors from all areas of the country. I also sat in on a forum in which APS workers talked about what worked best in the fight against elder abuse in each of their states.

There were many points of agreement. All of them felt the states should equalize definitions of both "elderly" and "abuse" in their statutes so that there could be an agreed-upon national policy. All of them agreed that incompetency proceedings must be improved across the board. All of them agreed the most effective way to deal with financial exploitation of the elderly is to connect the many different social-service agencies within the community: the bankers, doctors, psychiatrists, real estate agents, attorneys, stockbrokers, and law enforcement personnel. Each state that had already implemented such multidisciplinary anti-elder abuse teams reported resounding successes both in stopping the abuse and in more rapidly resolving abuse cases one by one.

Adult Protective Services workers are fighting on the front lines every day. They begin the investigation files of elder-abuse cases, and many spoke of their frustration when their cases go ignored. APS workers from many states said they have to "babysit" each case. "You have to babysit a case to make sure the person at the next desk picks up the file and deals with it," they agreed. "You especially have to babysit a case when it goes to the D.A.'s office, because the D.A. won't make it a high priority otherwise," they agreed emphatically.

In talking about the multi-disciplinary approach in complicated financial exploitation cases, they all agreed. "Our work would be so much easier if we knew everything about law enforcement and if we were trained attorneys, or if we had real estate licenses. We just can't know it all, so we need members of the community to offer their expertise," said an APS supervisor from Atlanta.

Different laws in different states are helpful in righting financial wrongs done to elders. For example, Robin Bickford does estate management for the Bureau of Elder and Adult Services in Maine. She cited Maine's "Improvident Transfers Act," a real estate statute that allows easier prosecution and immediate transfer of property back to the elder. Under this statute, if you can prove that the victim was incapacitated and that the person who transferred property out of the victim's name had full trust of the victim and took advantage of that trust, the property is automatically transferred back to the victim.

Other APS workers, on hearing about the Improvident Transfers Act, grew very excited, because all of them had had terrible problems when dealing with elders whose assets had been taken across state lines into other districts. When a perpetrator takes assets out of state, APS has to hire an attorney in the other state, as well as a private investigator. Often, litigation must take place more than once, in more than one state. The Improvident Transfers Act, if implemented across the country, might save a lot of this complicated hassle.

Everyone agreed that banks must become more involved in the fight against elderly exploitation. Banks across the country are getting sued for allowing obvious exploiters to forge checks, take over home loans, sign loans against elderly clients' homes, etc. Many states mandate that banks must report any party they suspect of financially exploiting an elder; failure to do so results in criminal penalties. It behooves them, then, to gain awareness, so banks in many areas of the country have started training programs put on by APS.

Many heads nodded in agreement when an APS worker from Louisiana expressed frustration with law enforcement. "They still see elder abuse as a civil matter. I think we need to expand domestic violence laws to be more inclusive of elder abuse so that law enforcement acts. It is a criminal offense—taking someone's money is taking their money!"

The abuse of the power of attorney is a nationwide problem. A lot of elders don't understand how much authority they're giving away when they sign a power of attorney document. Many studies are now being conducted on power-of-attorney abuse. POA procedures clearly need changing, and in the next few years there will be changes.

In state courts, cases are delayed and delayed again. New attorneys constantly plead "ignorance of case," and a case can be stayed twenty times. Nevada has an expedited trials law, especially where elderly victims are involved, and judges can put defendants in jail without bail. In Florida and California, when the victims are very ill or elderly their testimony can be videotaped. As long as the videotape includes a cross-examination by the opposing attorney, the videotape can be used in court. In California, a new law states that if an elderly victim of financial abuse dies before the trial ends, the attorneys can still collect their fees. This gives more incentive to attorneys to prosecute such cases.

I spoke in depth with Paul Cirincione, an APS specialist in Florida. Florida has a mandatory reporting requirement whereby anyone working with the elderly must report suspected elder abuse. Doctors, senior housing employees, bank officials, and law-enforcement officers are especially mandated. Failure to report is a crime.

"In Florida, we also have an 800-number hotline where anybody suspecting elder abuse can call in anonymously, even without first-hand knowledge. As a consequence, 20,000 cases a year get investigated, and this is all under a civil law that doesn't require proof of willful intent. Now, some people have a problem with this, but the burden of proof in a civil case requires only a preponderance of evidence, whereas in a criminal case, it's harder—it must be proven beyond a reasonable doubt. Either way, in Florida it's almost impossible to prosecute exploitation cases. Our law has no teeth against non-professional abusers. Caregivers to the elderly are screened very carefully, and if they are found guilty of elder abuse at any time, it goes on their permanent records for fifty years. That's effective, and so now we're changing the law so that it can be more effective against non-professional abusers. I'm on the committee that's pushing for the changes in the next legislative session."

Another Florida APS worker trying to change Florida's laws on elder abuse is Margaret Dixon. Margaret Dixon is a medical health care program specialist with APS, and she met with the State Senate to complain about the wording in elder abuse laws. The wording in the elder financial abuse statute was changed six months ago from "the improper use of assets" to "the illegal use of assets." What that did, according to Ms. Dixon, is get a lot of cases transferred directly to law enforcement, "and they don't prosecute because incapacitated people make very bad witnesses in court. If they do prosecute, they're not trained to look out for the welfare of the elderly, which is our main concern at APS."

I asked Dixon if there were any recent improvements in prosecution rates for financial abuse of the elderly and she said, "Our new law has new penalties. It's stricter, more specific. It requires APS to tell police immediately when they begin to investigate. The State Attorney's office is immediately notified, and that's gotten good results: lots of prosecutions by the State Attorney."

"Would you say that prosecution rates are better in the very wealthy sections of Florida?"

"Yes, I would. Ft. Lauderdale, West Palm Beach, also St. Petersburg. Law enforcement there is very attuned to financial exploitation of the elderly. The prosecution rates are very high. Yes, the rich do get taken care of better that way. I work in the north of Florida, and there aren't as many reports. We can always improve, you know, no matter what."

The third APS supervisor I spoke with works at the other end of the country, in Los Angeles. He is John P. Coyle, a Human Services Administrator specializing in planning and program development. He has been working with APS for twenty years, and he says, "I can really believe in this program."

I asked him when emphasis on financial elder abuse began.

"About 1984, when elder abuse awareness rode piggyback with spouse abuse awareness. Mandatory reporting by health practitioners, care custodians, educational facilities, and law enforcement has made a big difference in the number of reports. Now about 25% of the elder abuse reports we get are financial. That number has levelled off, but the public-awareness campaign has really paid off."

"How successful are you in getting cases solved?"

"I'd say we're 100% successful about half the time."

"Tell me how the process works in the most successful cases."

"Well, our hotlines are open twenty-four hours a day, seven days a week. We get to cases as fast as possible, and if there's immediate danger, we act. We try to get our cases solved within forty-five days. With financial abuse, we connect immediately with our task force, FAST— the Fiduciary Abuse Specialist Team—and they get to work. The team is composed of APS workers, law enforcement, gerontology psychiatrists, attorneys, and many other members of the business community. They review the case together and decide on action. We've had great success with that program, and I'm especially proud because I helped start FAST."

What all APS workers across the country have in common is relentless, extremely hard work.

Interview with A. Paul Blunt, an Arizona Attorney Specializing in Elderly Exploitation Cases

Paul Blunt has been an attorney for fourteen years, but for the last five years he has been, in his own words, "one hundred percent specialized in fiduciary abuse litigation." He has written several articles on fiduciary abuse of the elderly, and has worked closely with the National Center on Elder Abuse in Washington, D.C. He has addressed the Adult Protective Services conference for the last four years. His approach to the crime of financial exploitation is tough, aggressive, and far-reaching. What may emerge as his most important contribution to the successful prosecution of exploiters in the civil realm is his focus on banks' culpability.

In an article Blunt wrote for *Frontline* magazine, his position was made clear. "Banks are in a unique position to report suspected financial exploitation, since they have responsibility for holding the adult's financial assets. Even in the thirty-one states where such reports are optional, statutes clearly include banks as one of the groups that may report suspected exploitation. The penalties for failure to report can be severe. In more than thirty states, failure to report will subject the non-reporting party to criminal misdemeanor liability. However, beyond potential criminal liability, banks have a far greater concern in terms of civil liability." Blunt has also been involved with educational programs instructing banks on their duties and liabilities. I interviewed him in San Antonio, Texas, and asked about his personal experiences with elderly exploitation cases.

"What realities do you face in civil exploitation cases?"

"The first reality is that it costs me $30,000–$50,000 in lawyer's fees to do a case, so there has to be compensation. Pure economics: it has to be big enough to make it worth my while as well as the victim's. Fiduciary abusers are very bad with money, and they always have been. Most of them have no other financial means of support. Fifteen percent of them have drinking problems, and 10% of them have drug problems. When they take Granny's money, it's gone, so I need a secondary source of collectibility. If I can prove that the bank, for example, had every reason to suspect exploitation but failed to report, I will consider them as a collectable source, not only for the actual damages resulting from the illegal transfer, but potentially for the elder's mental anguish, attorney's fees, interest, and court costs.

"I also tell the victim up front that I can't rely on him to help himself or herself. I won't represent the victim. I tell the victim to go into conservatorship, and I represent the conservatorship."

"How do your exploitation trials begin?"

"I go before the probate judge and slap a suit on the perpetrator.

I tell the judge he needs to freeze all the assets of the defendant because I believe I can prove that these assets were obtained through fraud and elderly fiduciary abuse. When I get this freeze, the other lawyer suddenly produces bank account numbers that would take months to investigate."

"Can you talk in general about the biggest problems in combating the crime of financial abuse of the elderly, as well as your feelings on the best ways to fight the crime?"

"The biggest problem is that elderly financial abuse frequently goes unreported. A recent study in Canada suggested that fiduciary abuse is the most widespread form of elderly abuse, yet only one in twenty-five victims reports it. Often the victim is too tied to the abuser emotionally, physically, and financially. Especially if they're incapacitated. Furthermore, the D.A.s and police departments are not interested in prosecution of these crimes. Their focus is on violent crimes. Of the cases that were reported in this study, not one case was prosecuted. Rectification is not happening. Social complacency is probably the biggest key to fighting abuse against the elderly. When the public demands that the problem be solved, it will be solved."

"And the solutions?"

"My battle plan comes from *The Art of War* by Sun Tsu. Create alliances. Make your army bigger than theirs. Multi-disciplinary teams are essential, composed of many social service agencies, law enforcement, and the private sector. Develop specialty fiduciary abuse teams that are focused and expert. Specialization is always more efficient."

"Can you give me an example of a civil fiduciary elder abuse case you won recently?"

"Yes, and this one is fairly typical. An old couple in their eighties with no kids had outlived their relatives. They both had cancer, and they'd lived in their home for the last sixty years. They had $250,000 in cash. When the husband was in the hospital, an electrical contractor and his family befriended the wife. Over a period of months, she was undergoing surgery and radiation treatment for her cancer. The electrician's family drove her to treatments, and so forth.

"After the husband died, she typed a check to the electrical contractor for $85,000. He obtained a power of attorney, then there were six more checks totalling $150,000. When she went to an attorney to have her will rewritten, the attorney became alarmed and turned the case over to me. We found all the signed checks, and I had the woman placed in conservatorship with a neighbor—we had the neighbor bonded. We found where the money had gone. The contractor had purchased land, so we transferred the big piece back to my client's name. We sold the smaller piece and got $150,000 back for her."

Interview with Marc B. Hankin, "Mr. Elder Law of California"

Marc Hankin is an attorney in Los Angeles whose tireless efforts on behalf of the elderly have resulted in the passage of major legislation. He is the father of Welfare and Institutions Code Section 14006.2, the California law that allows spouses to avoid nursing home impoverishment by dividing community property and gifting the home to the healthier spouse.

The first legislation of its type, that vitally important law has been copied in many states. A modified version became federal law in 1988. Hankin also drafted the Elder Abuse and Dependent Adult Civil Protection Act (EADACPA), which California Governor Pete Wilson signed into law in 1991, and which enables abused seniors to sue their abusers. EADACPA requires the victimizer to pay for the successful senior's pain and suffering, even if the verdict of "guilty" is rendered after the victim's death. This has provided an important incentive for attorneys to prosecute elder abuse cases, as well as for victims to come forth; prior to passage of EADACPA, there was no award for pain and suffering.

Hankin is also an active member of the Los Angeles FAST—the highly successful multi-disciplinary team that combats fiduciary abuse.

"Mr. Hankin, in your opinion what is the key to fighting financial abuse of the elderly right now?"

"We must improve the definition of competence. One of the biggest problems in elder fiduciary abuse cases is the bad guys say, 'Hey, she was competent when she deeded her home to me, and even if she wasn't, how would I know?'"

"California's recently enacted Due Process in Competence Determination Act makes it possible in many cases to determine in an *objective* way that a victim lacked the legal mental capacity to make an apparent gift or contract. The Act was co-sponsored and jointly developed by the California State Bar Association's Estate Planning Trust and Probate Law Section and the California Medical Association. The new law establishes a forthright and functional definition of competence. It was very uplifting to be working in such close collaboration with highly gifted and idealistic but realistic professionals from two traditional enemy camps, lawyers and doctors, all working for the same altruistic objectives."

"What about legislation enabling banks to put a temporary hold on the funds of an obviously incompetent person?"

"I am working on a proposal to allow a bank to hold funds, provided that a police officer supports the hold with an affadavit that a crime is being committed against the incompetent victim."

"I understand you're working on another potential law."

"It's an amendment to EADACPA, whereby 20% of post-death recoveries would go into a revolving fund rather than to the plaintiffs. Five percent would go to prosecutors to enable them to hire forensic experts and other special professional witnesses to help their case. Another 5%–10% would go to a special department of the Attorney General, who would investigate allegations of abuses in conservatorships in different counties. The remaining money would go into computerization and a huge database, and possibly some money would go to the senior center that reported the abuse, as an award and incentive. These are all just ideas now, but some legislators' staffs are interested in developing them into workable law."

"Can you tell me about the database you have in mind?"

"The database would link probate courts with Adult Protective Services, Senior Ombudsmen, and the Department of Health Services investigative staff. There has to be a more integrated network of social services, and this would facilitate that."

"Have you worked with the D.A.'s office on elderly fiduciary abuse cases?"

"Yes. They are prosecuting and I am suing a preacher who got a woman to deed her home to him to thank him for his preacher visits. She was incapacitated."

"How do you feel about tougher sentences for crimes against the elderly?"

"Severity of punishment is not a deterrent. The probability of punishment is. Also, there has to be more restitution in these cases, and you could bargain, saying 'You'll get fifteen years instead of five unless you make restitution.'"

"Do you have any ideas about how you or I might prevent getting taken in our old age?"

"I was thinking about it. If you have a group of lifelong friends whom you trust and who know you better than anyone, they should be the group who decides when you are suffering from a mental or physical disease and are in danger of losing your assets. It would be agreed in advance that they would go to a judge and declare you incompetent. You could protest their judgement, but the judge would have to find that your lifelong friends are clearly wrong, if you opt into that system while you are still clearly competent. You need to have a tax estate planner. That's it."

Interview with Susan Aziz, Coordinator of FAST

Susan Aziz is known throughout the country for the work she is doing in the fight against financial exploitation of the elderly. She works tirelessly; I interviewed her for three hours, from ten in the morning until one in the afternoon. She is tall, slender, and calm, considering all the programs she organizes and all the people she is constantly connecting. Rather than a question-answer session, Susan provided an overview, and I came away amazed by the breadth of her experience. Her insights into the "big picture" of financial exploitation of the elderly encompass all aspects of the problem.

Aziz's compassion for the elderly grew from her personal experience. Her father was stricken with Alzheimer's disease, and was incapacitated for twenty years before his death. Fortunately for those she helps, her compassion is matched by her extremely efficient practicality. She acts.

Aziz is a consultant for WISE Senior Services, which developed and managed the Elder Abuse Prevention Project for Los Angeles. WISE coordinates the award-winning multi-disciplinary team in Los Angeles known as the Fiduciary Abuse Specialist Team (FAST). FAST is a model program being emulated across the country to fight financial abuse of the elderly, and Aziz is the coordinator of the team and chairs each meeting. She seems to know everyone in the country who is doing innovative things to stop the plunder.

Aziz began by telling me about a case worked on by the FAST team in which an elderly man in his eighties complained that his daughter had looted his safe-deposit box and possibly forged a grant deed. The man seemed very fearful of his daughter; he was afraid she would poison him. FAST recommended that a conservator be appointed to protect the man, and that a criminal investigation be implemented. Charges under the penal code—violation of a caretaker's trust—were subsequently brought against the daughter. The man refused to cooperate with any further investigation, however, so the case had to be dropped.

"This is common," Aziz explained. In "family matter" crimes—elder abuse, child abuse, and domestic violence—there is often the problem of victims refusing to cooperate with agencies trying to help. Many elderly people are dependent on their families. There's so much fear, humiliation, and guilt mixed in there.

"It's different from child abuse. Elders usually have assets. They are voting adults. They have the right to self-determination, the right to poor judgement, and the right to folly. They can choose to stay in an abusive situation. In this case, if the man is not a threat to himself, you cannot force him to do what he doesn't want to do."

One frequent strategy is to recommend appointment of a conservator. In fact, when a private conservator is taking advantage of an elderly person, the probate court can establish a temporary public conservator to safeguard the elderly person's assets. Aziz went on to describe such a case, in which a son who was his mother's private conservator was not making her mortgage payments or paying her utility bills. She faced foreclosure, and her son was planning to sell her home to a friend—probably not with his mother's best interests in mind. The FAST team met and recommended that the Public Guardian petition the probate court. A temporary public conservatorship was established by the probate court, and the son ran, scared. Everyone cooperated; utility payments were made, and the house was taken out of foreclosure. The temporary conservator took action to sell the home so that the woman could get her equity out of the sale.

Among the ways elderly persons are exploited, a common scenario occurs when an abuser, who has convinced the elder to add his or her name to the property title, takes out huge loans against the equity in the elder's home. When the elder can't possibly make the payments, he or she loses the home in foreclosure. She went on to tell of many such cases, some of which I've presented in the section on home equity fraud. She then told me of a real eye-opening case, one she says she always uses when giving seminars on preventing financial abuse:

A man in his eighties with good mental capacity had two homes on one lot. He was married, so he and his wife lived in one home, and his daughter and son-in-law lived in the other home. His daughter convinced him to deed both houses to her, so that he'd no longer have to be responsible for taxes and maintenance. The agreement was that the daughter would stay in one house and the parents would live rent-free in the other until they died. They sold the two homes to the daughter for one half of their market value. He took money from the sale and gave an "early inheritance" to his other children as well.

When he was down to his last $1,000 the daughter served her own father and step-mother with a thirty-day eviction notice. She wanted to get rental income from the second house. His daughter had taken big loans against the equity in the property and had developed credit problems.

The father had a verbal contract with his daughter and his wife, in which his daughter had said he could live in the house until he died. The APS caseworker intervened and convinced the daughter to abide by the verbal contract. And the father was lucky, because in other similar cases the home is gone and the elderly victim has no place to go.

Aziz said she thinks many elders don't realize how much longer they have to live. People are living longer than they ever expected to, and they need to have some money at the end of their lives.

Aziz also had some great boyfriend/girlfriend cases, and they all basically went like this: an elderly woman or an elderly man was spending a lot of time alone, when along came a much younger—as much as forty years younger—"friend" of the opposite sex, and the new friend spent quality time with the elderly person. They became closer, and the younger boyfriend or girlfriend started draining the bank account.

In cases such as these, Aziz explained, the FAST team's recommendation to the caseworker may be to contact the elderly person's family and get them involved if they have the elder's best interest at heart. You have to replace the victim's "love interest" with something—family love. They've found in some cases that if the family gets really involved, they replace the abuse with genuine loving concern. The victim will gravitate toward the real thing, and then contact with the abuser can be cut off.

I asked Aziz to summarize her vision about diminishing the threat of financial abuse, and she had a lot to say. "First of all, I need to say that financial abuse can be life-threatening. And almost always there is no way to recover financially, because most elderly persons are no longer in the workforce. Anyone entering the workforce should immediately start thinking about financial and estate planning. Work on it now, so that in the event that you do become incapacitated, provisions for managing your finances and care are made. A car can hit you tomorrow, rendering you incapable of making a decision about financial, legal, and health-care planning. Make directives for health care. The durable power of attorney for health care only kicks in when you become incapacitated. Make legal and financial provisions in case you someday lose capacity. Be careful of whom you trust. Many people give away assets because they didn't think they'd live so long. Be financially prepared to live a very long time."

Aziz became more passionate as she said, "We are our brother's keeper. We have no mandated reporting laws for financial abuse in California, but if you're a bank employee or a relative or a friend, and you suspect that an elderly person is being financially exploited, report these suspicions to Adult Protective Services or to the Long-Term Ombudsman in the area. In California, voluntary reporting on elderly fiduciary abuse goes to either APS or the Ombudsman or to law enforcement. The current law does provide voluntary reporters with protection from liability as long as the report is made in good faith.

"Also, if you have an elderly person as a relative or close friend, do not let him or her become isolated. Stay in touch, and stay involved. If you are retired, don't let yourself become isolated. Join senior centers, clubs, or other groups. The mere presence of other people helps to protect you and enriches your life.

"Everyone should be aware of the abuse indicators." (I mentioned them in the "Abuse Signals" section.) "Educate yourself, and be alert. If you're suspicious, report, report, report."

Multi-Disciplinary Teams and How They Operate

In cities throughout the country, social service workers have joined with law enforcement and various consultants in the private sector to fight fiduciary abuse of the elderly. In South Carolina, Arizona, Georgia, and Illinois, for example, Adult Protective Services workers regularly train all levels of bank employees in educational seminars on financial abuse of the elderly. Banks are then represented by these educated employees, who join the multi-disciplinary team along with law-enforcement agents, gerontologists, psychiatrists, and attorneys. The teams avoid bureaucratic wastes of time, like repeating the story and file over and over. One multi-disciplinary team confronts and solves the case rapidly. As the cases are usually complex, the expertise of many sectors is required; when the many sectors all sit in the same room, an enormous block of time is saved.

Fiduciary abuse cases are complex, partly because of the nature of the transactions involved. For example, the abuse could include transfer of a deed to real estate as well as the cashing of bearer bonds. The abuser has often been committing the abuse over a long period of time, and bank records and other documents can be very difficult to obtain. The victim's competence level—both now and when the abuse occurred—must be ascertained. There is no way the Adult Protective Services worker assigned to a financial abuse case could be trained in all these areas! That's why the multi-disciplinary team was developed.

I have chosen to describe the operational procedure of the multidisciplinary Los Angeles Fiduciary Abuse Specialist Team (FAST), because it is exemplary. The FAST coordinator has presented at conferences in several states interested in the FAST model. Fast has been highly successful; since the team began meeting in 1993—two years ago at this writing—FAST has provided in-depth consultation on forty-two cases, as well as numerous telephone consultations for emergency situations.

All the FAST consultants provide their services without pay. They join the team by signing a Memorandum of Understanding, in which they agree to provide their professional opinion and advice at the monthly team meetings and by telephone on an emergency basis, to attend an orientation session, and, when possible, to educate other professionals and the public about how to recognize, stop, and prevent financial abuse. Expert consultation is provided to local APSs, ombudsmen, public guardians, and other case workers. Team members include seventeen APS workers, ombudsmen, PG "fiduciary abuse specialists," and over twenty consultants, including six lawyers (two District Attorneys, one City Attorney, one Public Counsel, one in legal aid and one in private practice), one geriatrician, three representatives of case management programs, one private conservator, one real-estate broker, one vice president of a bank, four representatives of law enforcement (two city and two county), one stockbroker who also has expertise in insurance, one geriatric psychiatrist with expertise in determining mental capacity, and one retired commissioner from the County of Los Angeles Superior Court. There are also back-up consultants and guest consultants whose expertise is especially useful for particular cases. A typical meeting is attended by thirty-five to forty-five people. Susan Aziz is the chairperson, and the APS, ombudsman, and PG administrators facilitate the case consultations.

During the first year of operation, there was a team-oriented session and a training program of five half-days aimed at all APS, ombudsmen, and case workers. Topics covered were "How to Recognize and Investigate Cases of Fiduciary Abuse," "How to Recognize and Stop the Loss of Real Property," "How to Gather Evidence of Incompetence of Conservatorship and Lawsuits," "How to Stop the Loss of Liquid Assets," and "Investigative Interviewing and Recording." Training has also been provided to over 1,250 bankers and fraud investigators throughout California.

Meetings last three hours, and two new cases are handled at each meeting. The FAST team's success demonstrates how—to use Paul Blunt's terminology—we can make our army larger and more powerfully effective.

Conclusions:
More Solutions and More Resources

So how do we curb the fastest growing crime in America? Throughout this book I've given the opinions of experts from all over the country. Educating potential victims to protect themselves before they become targets is essential. Different states' attacks on the crisis provide lessons for other states to follow. In Nevada, for example, crimes against those over sixty-five bring "double time," or twice the jail time as crimes against those under sixty-five.

Elder law in America is in a period of transition, and changes yet to come in the field will mean vast improvements in the quality of life for older Americans. It is vital that more attorneys throughout the country specialize in elder law. In the 1994-95 edition of the *Martindale–Hubbel Law Directory*, only twelve attorneys practicing law in the United States include elder law in the description of their fields of expertise: one attorney in Florida, one in Arizona, one in San Francisco, and nine in Southern California. That number must grow, and for it to grow there must be incentive for these attorneys to prosecute on behalf of victims of fiduciary abuse of the elderly.

Paul Blunt is one of the twelve. He practices in Arizona, and he has been aggressively successful, winning large awards from secondary sources in civil cases of fiduciary abuse of the elderly. Blunt hopes to get banks, along with other large professional institutions across the country, more involved in protecting elderly clients' assets. He believes that instilling the fear of lawsuits is one way to do it.

In a landmark case in Florida, one bank was made to pay. This could be a start in getting banks to become involved in the fight against financial abuse of the elderly. The case was Republic National Bank of Miami vs. Maria Johnson. Maria Johnson was a frail woman in her seventies who suffered from dementia to the point where she was incapable of carrying on a normal conversation. She had an account with Republic National Bank totalling $60,000, and she'd held the account with the bank for a long time.

During a period of fourteen days in 1989, Maria Johnson withdrew all of that $60,000. Tragically, it turns out that she was probably a kidnap victim. Immediately before the withdrawals began, she'd been married. The manager of the building where she lived testified that

Ms. Johnson appeared before him during those fourteen days with a woman who would not allow her to speak.

Many bank tellers testified on the witness stand, saying Maria Johnson's circumstances should have raised immediate red flags on her account: sudden substantial withdrawal activity on an older person's account where there had been none previously is something all tellers are trained to observe. The fact that Maria Johnson seemed agitated and disoriented was another red flag, they testified. Yet the tellers ignored these red flags they'd all been trained to observe. The court's decision that the bank was negligent was affirmed.

The substantial award given Ms. Johnson is important, because professional institutions can no longer shirk their duties to their older clients. Whether in telemarketing crimes, theft of bank assets, or bank loans placed on victims in home-equity scams, banks can no longer claim immunity. They can no longer profit from the fleecing of older Americans, because attorneys will nail them for substantial damages. The banking community in America is a huge entity that can no longer be allowed to profit from the fleecing. They must watch out now for their older clients. This participation will go a long way toward combatting the problem.

Finally, if crimes against the elderly are to cease, attitudes toward older citizens must change. When older people are no longer seen as vulnerable easy targets, crimes against them will cease. When older people are seen and treated as the vital, precious resources they truly are, crimes against them will cease. When criminals understand that the public will not allow them to abuse their parents and grandparents, crimes against the elderly will cease. When the public demands that law enforcement no longer allow abuse against the elderly to go unpunished, crimes against them will cease.

To grow old means to have seen and survived a great deal. Old people are tough. In this brutal world, however, they must get tougher. They must recognize themselves as vital, precious resources, and in a loud, united voice, demand their rights.

Appendix

Adult Protective Services is the agency to call if you have experienced elder abuse yourself or suspect abuse elsewhere. If you look in your local phone book in the government pages or the community services pages, you may see the following headings: Department of Aging, Division of Aging, or Area Agency on Aging. These are good general resource centers, and if you call them they will direct you to the right APS office. At the back of this book you'll find state agencies on aging for every state in America. Call the number listed to find the APS office in your area. In the government pages of your telephone book under "Social Services" there should be a phone number for the Adult Protective Services office in your area. Adult Protective Services is equipped to handle all complaints of elder abuse, so if you or someone you know is being abused—or if you have reason to believe so, but are not sure there is abuse—APS will go into action. If you or someone you know is in immediate danger, they will work with law enforcement to get you out of danger immediately.

If you feel you have been fleeced and you want some legal advice, look for a listing in the government section of your phone book for "Seniors, Legal Aid" or "Senior Law Center" or something similar. By calling that local number, you will be directed to someone who specializes in legal matters pertaining to seniors. Or you can call your local AARP chapter if you're a member, and ask what they recommend.

Where to Go If You Are Being Abused by Family Members

AARP Grandparent Information Center
Social Outreach and Support Section
601 E Street NW; Washington, DC, 20049
(202) 434-2296

Coalition for Grandparents Parenting Grandchildren
Center on Aging
140 Earl Warren Hall; University of California; Berkeley, CA, 94720
(510) 643-6427

GASP (Grandparents as Second Parents)
#10 Eastmont Mall, Suite 8; Oakland, CA, 94605
(510) 568-7786

National Coalition of Grandparents (NCOG)
137 Larkin Street; Madison, WI, 53705
(608) 238-87851

ROCK (Raising Our Children's Kids)
Post Office Box 96; Niles, MI, 49120
(616) 683-9038

Grandparents Who Care
San Francisco General Hospital
Post Office Box 24576; San Francisco, CA, 94124
(415) 644-4757 or (415) 822-4457

State Agencies on Aging

The offices listed below coordinate services for older Americans. They may be used as great starting places, as they provide information on services, programs, and opportunities for older Americans. I've listed only the phone numbers, which should be toll-free in your state. Where there may be a charge, I've listed the toll-free 800 number, which will be free. "TDD" refers to Telecommunication Devices for the Deaf; these numbers are equipped to handle people with speech or hearing impairments.

Alabama ....(205) 242-5743 or (800) AGELINE
Alaska ....(907) 465-3250
American Samoa ..011 (684) 633-1251
Arizona ....(602) 542-4446
Arkansas ....(501) 682-2441 or (800) 482-8049
California ....(916) 322-5290; TDD: (916) 323-8913
　　　　　　　　　or (800) 231-4024
Colorado ....(303) 866-5800
Connecticut .....(203) 566-3238; TDD: (800) 443-9946
Delaware ....(302) 577-4791 or (800) 223-9074
Dist. of Columbia .(202) 724-5623
Florida ....(904) 488-8922
Georgia ....(404) 894-5333
Guam ....(671) 632-4141 or (671) 632-4153
Hawaii ....(808) 586-0100 or (800) 468-4644
Idaho ....(208) 334-3833
Illinois ....(217) 785-2870; TDD: (800) 252-8966
Indiana ....(317) 232-7020 or (800) 545-7763
Iowa ....(515) 281-5187; TDD: (515) 281-5188
　　　　　　　　　or (800) 532-3213
Kansas ....(913) 296-4986 or (800) 432-3535
Kentucky ....(502) 564-6930; TDD: (502) 564-5497
　　　　　　　　　or (800) 372-2973
Louisiana ....(504) 925-1700
Maine ....(207) 624-5335
Maryland ....(410) 225-1100 or (800) 243-3425;
　　　　　　　　　TDD: (410) 383-7555

Massachusetts .... (617) 727-7750 or (800) 882-2003;
TDD: (800) 922-2275
Michigan .... (517) 373-8230
Minnesota .... (612) 296-2770 or (800) 882-6262
Mississippi .... (601) 359-6770 or (601) 359-6703
or (800) 345-6347
Missouri .... (314) 751-8535 or (800) 392-0210
Montana .... (406) 444-4204 or (800) 332-2272
Nebraska .... (402) 471-2306
Nevada .... (702) 486-3545
New Hampshire ... (603) 271-4680 or (800) 351-1888
New Jersey .... (609) 292-4833 or (800) 792-8820
New Mexico ...... (505) 827-7640 or (800) 432-2080
New York .... (518) 474-4425 or (800) 342-9871
North Carolina .... (919) 733-3983; TDD: (800) 662-7030
North Dakota ..... (701) 224-2577 or (800) 755-8521
Ohio .... (614) 466-5500 or (800) 282-1206;
TDD: (614) 466-6191
Oklahoma .... (405) 521-2327; TDD: (405) 521-2328
Oregon .... (503) 378-4728 or (800) 282-8096;
TDD: (800) 232-3020
Pennsylvania ..... (717) 783-1550
Puerto Rico ...... (809) 721-4560
Rhode Island ..... (800) 322-2880; TDD: (401) 277-2880
South Carolina .... (803) 735-0210 or (800) 868-9095
South Dakota ..... (605) 773-3656
Tennessee .... (615) 741-2056
Texas .... (512) 444-2727 or (800) 252-9240
Utah .... (801) 538-3910
Vermont .... (802) 241-2400
Virgin Islands ..... (809) 774-0930
Virginia .... (800) 552-4464; TDD: (804) 225-2271
Washington ...... (206) 493-2509 or (800) 422-3263
West Virginia ..... (304) 558-3317
Wisconsin .... (608) 266-2536
Wyoming .... (307) 777-7986 or (800) 442-2766

Bibliography

"Abusing the Elderly." *Newsweek*, September 1985.

"The CPS Experience." *Public Welfare*, Spring 1988.

FDCH Congressional Testimony, September 28, 1994, page 8, "William J. Esposito, Deputy Assistant Director, Federal Bureau of Investigation, House Small Business Telemarketing Fraud."

National Health Care Anti-Fraud Association. "Fact Sheet, 1994." 1994.

National Health Care Anti-Fraud Association. "Guidelines to Health Care Fraud Adopted by the NHCAA Board of Governors, 1991." 1991.

National Health Care Anti-Fraud Association. "Prison Time, Heavy Fines Ordered for Two in Rolling Labs Case." *Network*, vol. IV, no. 1, November 1994.

National Health Care Anti-Fraud Association. "U.S. Health Care Spending and the Impact of Health Care Fraud." 1993.

Phillips, Guy Ragland. *Brigantia*. London: Routledge and Kegan Paul, 1976.

Scot, Reginald. *Discoverie of Witchcraft*. Yorkshire, England: Rowmand & Littlerfield, 1973.

State of California Health and Welfare Agency, "Table 10, Types of Confirmed Elder (65+) Abuse Perpetrated by Others, 1993."

State of Nevada Division for Aging Services, Elder Abuse Reporting System, Complaint Data by County, 1993 and 1994.

Steinmetz, S.K. "Elder Abuse." *Aging*, January-February 1981.

Taeuber, Cynthia. *Sixty-Five Plus in America*. U.S. Department of Commerce, Economics and Statistics Administration, Bureau of the Census, 1992.

Tatara, Toshio. "Elder Abuse in the United States: An Issue Paper." National Aging Resource Center on Elder Abuse, August 1990.

Tatara, Toshio. "Summaries of National Elder Abuse Data: An Exploratory Study of State Statistics Based on a Survey of State APS and Aging Agencies." National Aging Resource Center on Elder Abuse, Washington, DC, February 1980.

United States Congress. *Congressional Record—Senate*. March 11, 1993: page S2792, remarks by Mr. Bryan; page S2794, remarks by Mr. McCain.